The Missing BEAUMONT CHILDREN

50 years of
Mystery and Misery

MICHAEL MADIGAN

First published by Elvis Press 2015
Copyright © Michael Madigan 2015

ISBN 9780975674673

All rights reserved. No part of this book may be reproduced or transmitted by any person or entity, including internet search engines or retailers, in any form or by any means, electronic or mechanical, including photocopying (except under the statutory exceptions provisions of the Australian Copyright Act 1968), recording, scanning or by any information storage and retrieval system without permission of the author.

Cover design: Luke Harris, WorkingType Studio
Editor: Avylon Magarey

This book is dedicated to
Nancy and Grant Beaumont
Rest in peace Jane, Arnna and Grant

Acknowledgement

I would like to thank my loving family for their constant love and support, especially my wife Marty who never complains about the many hours I have spent glued to my keyboard.

To our two beautiful daughters Avy (editor) and Bonnie, and my wonderful son Viv, thanks for your love and encouragement.

My parents Ken and Margaret are inspirational. Their guidance and love has given me strength.

To my sisters Sharon, Cathy, Angela and Lizzy and brother Anthony, as well as my extended family of Rhodrey, Angus, Callum, Rhiannon and 'Prince' Ashton, I love you all so much.

This book has relied heavily on the work of dozens of skilled journalists and authors, many of whom are no longer with us; thank you for your skillful reporting.

A special thank you goes to Graham Archer of the Seven Network for not only kindly providing images for this book but also for his support in my endeavours over many years.

Contents

Prelude

PART ONE — Three Children are Missing

Chapter 1	Grant and Nancy	16
Chapter 2	"It's all My Fault"	29
Chapter 3	The Man with the Crazy Walk	52
Chapter 4	False Hope	65
Chapter 5	1966 — The Year of Lost Children	76
Chapter 6	Paranormal Detectives	81
Chapter 7	The One Pound Note	101
Chapter 8	'There is someone out there'	107
Chapter 9	A Letter from 'Jane'	117
Chapter 10	Dead End	127

PART TWO — Two Children are Missing

Chapter 11	Joanne and Kirste	133
Chapter 12	Cluster Killings	163
Chapter 13	'Von Evil'	172
Chapter 14	"I found Jane Beaumont"	180
Chapter 15	Persons of Interest	189
Chapter 16	Satin Man	207
Chapter 17	What's New?	213
Chapter 18	Who Could Do Such a Thing?	224
Chapter 19	Gone but Never Forgotten	240
Reference		245
Index		249

Prelude

August 17, 1925
Melbourne

Geoffrey England (8) spent the morning at St Kilda Beach building sand castles and digging for elusive tiny mud crabs on the foreshore. He was not alone. Even though it was a cold winter's day the clear skies had enticed a crowd of people to Melbourne's most popular beach. Geoffrey was playing with other children without his parent's supervision; they were back at their two story mansion, one kilometre away.

When Geoffrey's stomach rumbled at around midday he wandered back to his home. Geoffrey's family lived along Kooyong Road, a well-to-do part of the city. His father Stanley was a respected Melbourne barrister. He and his sister attended the best private schools in Melbourne; and enjoyed a somewhat privileged life.

As he walked into his home he was greeted by his mother and father who were dressed in their finest outfits. His father looked dapper in a blue stripe suit with a top hat. His mother wore an impressive gown which 'ballooned' her petite figure.

"Come and have lunch Geoffrey, we're off to the races".

Geoffrey's eyes lit up.

"You and your sister are going to the moving pictures".

The little boy's eyes focused on the wooden floorboards.

"Can't I go back to the beach?"

Marjorie and Geoffrey waved their parents goodbye as the handsome couple took the tram into the centre of Melbourne. The two children then walked to the Malvern picture theatre and enjoyed the films. Immediately after, Geoffrey took his sisters hand and headed for the tram stop. The winter sun had just burst through the grey clouds; Geoffrey was adamant they were going to the beach. They caught the tram to St Kilda Beach and began playing with other children; however a young woman and a middle aged man soon befriended Geoffrey and Marjorie.

The man began showing the boy how to build a raft from old bits of wood that had washed up on the seashore. The woman took a shine to the girl. Together they walked along the long and rickety pier. The sea was rough with waves smashing onto the jetty's wooden pylons. Geoffrey found a length of old string and imagined he was fishing; the man stared at him, lost in thought.

Suddenly, Geoffrey asked the man for the time, as he wanted to be home before his parents.

"Quarter past four".

"Here, have this and go and buy some sweets".

The boy gazed at the shiny sixpence and rushed off to the corner deli close by and returned with a large bag of lollies.

The man then told him that Marjorie was going back into

town with him and his lady friend. "We are going to take her to tea and then to a dance show".

The man kissed Marjorie and the four walked towards the cable trams on the upper side of the esplanade. Marjorie was escorted onto the tram by the couple. The little girls face showed both excitement and apprehension. The man lent out of the tram and handed Geoffrey a shilling. "We will bring Marjorie home tonight. Meet us on the hill on Kooyong Road around 10 o'clock. Tell your parents that Marjorie had guests for the evening."

On the way home from the races, Mr and Mrs England got quite a shock when Geoffrey boarded their tram. "Where's Marjorie?"

That night police began a search both in the seaside neighbourhood and throughout the city.

Little Marjorie had been taken to the couple's home where she slept with them. In the morning she became frightened and cried; "I want to see mummy". The couple told her that she was going to stay with them *forever*.

When she realised she would not be going home she pleaded with them. The man and the women then argued. The woman wanted the girl to go home on a bus immediately; the man was adamant that he wanted the young girl to stay. He went to great pains to persuade the girl to live with them and become their daughter. He promised her all sorts of luxuries to entice her to stay but Marjorie did not budge. She also refused to eat the breakfast they had prepared for her which made the man angry. In desperation, he then offered Marjorie two shillings if she would just eat a slice of orange. "Eat it!" He yelled angrily. She pressed her lips tightly together. The woman then grabbed the girls arm and rushed out the front door onto the street. They ran into the centre of the city where Marjorie was given money to buy a tram ticket. She was home safe by midday.

Marjorie's story is just one of many incidents of child abduction in the early part of the twentieth century in Australia. Almost all abductions I have researched had relatively happy endings. The child has either escaped or was released. Very few cases went unsolved. The abduction and murder of a child was, and is still to this day extremely rare.

Child abduction throughout the history of Australia can be listed into five categories:
1. The 'stealing back' of a child who has been taken by government authorities due to welfare concerns.
2. The snatching of a baby, usually by a woman suffering from a mental illness.
3. Parental abduction. This is by far the most significant form of abduction in Australia and is generally caused by the unfortunate breakdown of the family unit.
4. The abduction of a child for ransom.
5. The abduction of a child by a sexual predator; 'stranger' abduction.

Abductions involving strangers, across all eras have a familiar ring to them. The crime is usually well planned, with the perpetrator frequently offering 'sweeteners' to endear themselves towards the young child or to catch them off guard.

The following cases show a distinct pattern used by perpetrators for over a century.

1929 — In the city of Albury, NSW, a girl (7) was playing with a group of children when she was asked by a man if she liked ice cream. She then accompanied him to a close-by paddock, where the man gave her a penny. Later she was found by a motorist on the side of a road, two miles from the town. A medical examination showed that she had been sexually violated.

1943 — A girl (4) was abducted from the front garden of her home in the Adelaide suburb of Joslin. The child, a daughter of a soldier was playing in a front garden when a man rode up on a bicycle. The child's grandmother who was sitting on the porch thought he was a friend until he swiftly lifted the child over the front gate and rode off with her. The girl was found several hours later, naked, running along a street with her clothes under her arm, crying.

1947 — A girl (6) was abducted by a man in Hindley Street, Adelaide, in broad daylight while her mother was talking to a friend. The girl was found half an hour later by a gardener at the Torrens Parade Ground.

The abduction took place while the children were looking in a shop window. They were approached by a man who then pointed to a weighing machine, "Come down and weigh yourselves."

The girl's brother (8) got on the scales and the man then lifted the girl on. The stranger then took the children down a lane. He gave the boy sixpence and said, "Wait here until we come back."

He then took the girl by the hand and walked off.

A gardener working on the lawns at the parade ground became suspicious of the man and challenged him. The perpetrator immediately ran away.

1953 — Fish and chips were on the dinner menu for two eight-year-old boys from Kent Town, an inner city suburb of Adelaide.

At 6.30 p.m. the boys, Kevin and Allan were walking to their local fish shop. Both of them were tightly gripping money and a list from their mums. They were stopped by a man walking in the opposite direction. The man stared into the eyes of Kevin as the boys tried to pass.

"Where are you going?"

"Fish-n-chip shop".

The man then grabbed Kevin by the hand who started to cry as he was dragged away.

After an intensive search the boy was located by police at 2.30 a.m. the following morning. The child was found asleep in bed with a man in a house at Brighton. The boy had suffered a terrifying experience, which culminated in a fight when the man (29) attacked the police after they had climbed through his bedroom window. During the night the man had taken the child to a party, passed him off as his son and had given him beer and wine to drink.

The man admitted to police that he took the child to sleep with and intended keeping him until "He did not want him anymore." He was charged with indecent assault and child abduction.

The abduction of children throughout the twentieth century was an ugly scourge on society, but a new level of deviancy was about to change the fabric of Australian society forever.

Part 1
Children Missing

1
Grant and Nancy

January 25, 1966

Grant Beaumont sat in his jade green Holden station wagon and watched with delight as his three children played on the cool grass along the foreshore of Glenelg Beach. He perspired from the early morning heat and wished he could stay with them; the sea looked enticingly flat, perfect for swimming. However, after four weeks of holidays it was time for Grant to return to work, as a traveling linen salesman.

Adelaide had experienced a prolonged 'hot spell' during January and to obtain relief, Grant and his children Jane, 9, Arnna, 7, and Grant Jnr. 4, had spent many wonderful days on the beach swimming and playing on the pristine white sands. They were not alone; every day during January, thousands of people had flocked to Adelaide's premier tourist destination.

Grant and his wife Nancy were fortunate to live only one and a half kilometres away at Harding Street, Somerton Park.

1 Grant and Nancy

On the beach Jane was busy organising her two younger siblings. Even at such a young age, she was described as being a 'motherly type'. Tall and slim, Jane was a reserved, intelligent girl who dreamed of becoming an author. She did wonderfully well at school, topping her class every year.

Arnna, personality wise, was the opposite of her sister. She was outgoing and affectionate; singing and dancing were her passions. She loved nothing better than playing 'dress-ups' for hours on end with her little brother and organising family concerts. Arnna lived in a delightful fantasy world.

Little Grant was happiest when following his father around the house or 'helping' his dad with car maintenance. When Grant Beaumont was at home his son was known as his 'little shadow'.

The 41-year-old father stayed for over half an hour at the beach, ensuring his children were safe and settled. He had informed them of the usual safety issues such as: 'not to go out too deep into the sea' and definitely 'do not talk to strangers'. Jane could swim a little and only ventured out as deep as her midriff; Arnna would only paddle in the shallows and little Grant would barely touch the water, before scampering back to the safety of the firm sand.

Grant watched his children incognito, but as the traveling salesman was about to turn the ignition key to start his journey, he noticed his son wave to him. The toddler ran over to the car. "Go on, Daddy. Don't worry, Daddy."

The last memory of his children was a happy one. They had struck up a friendship with other children and were playing and laughing together.

Grant Beaumont headed towards his destination, Snowtown,

a small rural town approximately 150 kilometres north of Adelaide in the heart of sheep grazing and wheat growing country. The unusual township name certainly did not come from climatic conditions; Sir Thomas Jervois (1878) named it as a gesture of gratitude to his aide de camp, Thomas Snow.

As Grant drove through the CBD of Adelaide, he passed the Torrens Parade Ground where council workers and young soldiers were preparing for Australia Day celebrations the following day.

The sight of the khaki uniforms reminded Grant of the time he served his country. In 1942, at the aged of 17 Grant had enlisted in the Army.

His military training began in the Adelaide Hills at the Woodside Army Barracks before crossing the border into the Victorian town of Watsonia. He then transferred to a 'young soldiers' battalion at French Forest in N.S.W. before going to the Canungra Jungle Training School in Queensland where he joined the 2/24 Infantry Battalion, 9th Division.

The 2/24th had earned a reputation as an elite fighting unit in the Middle East but were summoned back to Australia to face the Japanese threat in the Pacific. In April 1945 the 9th Division were sent to Morotai, a staging area, in preparation for the 7th and 9th Divisions' amphibious landings on Borneo. Extensive air and naval bombardment prior to the landing resulted in little opposition as the troops landed on the beaches. The two battalions then pushed inland towards the Tarakan township, where they overcame fierce Japanese resistance.

Grant Beaumont received a shrapnel injury in the battle at Tarakan and was flown back to Queensland for treatment. After the triumphant Allied victory, Grant volunteered for the

Occupation Forces unit in Japan where he spent two years guarding Japanese prisoners.

Grant finally returned to Adelaide a few days before the 1947 Anzac Day March. To his surprise his arrival had become newsworthy!

Unbeknown to Grant, his mother had gone to the Adelaide Railway Station on the previous six days, waiting patiently to welcome her son home. *The News* picked up on the story;

"A quiet little woman, dressed in black, went to platform 8 at the Adelaide Railway Station to meet the Melbourne Express, searching anxiously through the crowds, and walked away alone. Today her search had a happy ending. Her 22-year-old son, Private Grant Beaumont arrived back from Japan."

Grant's mother had not seen him for four years; she wept tears of joy when the two finally embraced. But his homecoming was also a sad one; his father had died only one month earlier.

After being discharged from the military, Grant, a qualified mechanic tried his hand in the taxi industry.

Grant (also known as Jim, a 'nickname' that stuck whilst in the Army) worked long hours to establish himself in the business which resulted in him owning a number of cabs at Suburban Taxis.

The trip to the mid-north of South Australia was slow as attached to the Holden was a caravan. Grant, Nancy and their children enjoyed many family trips around the state, as well as sojourns into Victoria to catch up with Army mates but the caravan became Grant's sleeping quarters and office when he was on the road meeting with clients. Grant arrived at Snowtown around midday. It was stinking hot and there didn't seem to be a soul in sight as he cruised down the main street. The paddocks surrounding the town were parched dry and strong northerly winds created 'wurleys' with the fine red sand. It was an unpleasant day.

Most of the clients he had planned to see were regrettably out of town and the customers he did meet that day were non-committal in regards to purchases. At 5 p.m., Grant, a little despondent from his meagre sales performance, returned to his caravan to cook himself some dinner.

Being a traveling salesman could be a demanding job but after hours the lifestyle became rather social. The 1960s produced a boom in salesmen visiting country towns where populations were increasing as the rural economy enjoyed a sudden growth in prosperity.

The country 'travelers' often bunked up in the local hotels which delighted the publicans as they would spend most of the nights drinking together. Grant wasn't one of them. He learnt at an early stage in his sales career that the money he made quickly slipped through his fingers at the front bar and so he always slept in his caravan away from temptation. He had the responsibility of his three children and a wife to support.

Grant was always keen to get out on the road working but missed his children greatly and his children missed him just as much. In his briefcase Grant carried letters his children often sent to him, and in the quiet of night he would read them. The most recent letter came from Jane.

"Dear Loving Daddy, when Auntie Talie came down to stay with us yesterday, we went to the Goodwood Pool last night.

Arnna and Grant swam in the toddlers' pool which was up to my waist on me, but Auntie, Mummy, and I swam in the 3 ft. 6 inch pool.

While we were there, I learnt how to open my eyes under the water for ever so long, and I learnt how to kick my legs and make my arms float, and dive, gracefully dive, racer's dive, and plain dive. I learnt all this from Auntie Talie.

There is only one thing I can't do, breathing out, as I am swimming along.

Tonight I had a hot pie, fritz and sauce sandwich, and rainbow ice-cream. Auntie Talie bought a great big roast chicken from her father for nothing!

Most of all, I want to wish you much luck with your hot, tiring work.

Well goodbye, I have to go now. I LOVE YOU."

Loving Jane xxxxxx

Grant carefully folded the letter back into the worn envelope and drifted off to sleep thinking of his three children.

January 26, 1966

At 7 a.m. Nancy Beaumont awoke to the sound of her two youngest children playing boisterously in the lounge room. It had been another warm summer's night, with an expected searing hot day ahead. The temperature was predicted to once again go past the 100°F mark.

Nancy Helen Ellis was born on August 5, 1927. She worked as a general office worker at the City Meat Company, North Adelaide when she met her handsome, husband-to-be Grant Beaumont.

In October 1955 Nancy dined out with her uncle and aunty

at the Victoria Hotel in Hindley Street, before heading off to the West's Cinema, situated across the street. Half-way through dinner, Grant walked in with a friend after having spent the day at the Balaklava races (90 km north of Adelaide). They had dropped into the hotel for celebratory drinks after backing a number of winners. Grant, with encouragement from his friend, plucked up the nerve to introduce himself to Nancy.

Grant fell in love at first sight; Nancy Ellis was an attractive, olive skinned young woman with a pretty face and large brown eyes. She had a sharp mind and a quick wit and loved having a laugh with her friends and workmates

The two got along well and a 'date' was organised for the following night. They enjoyed each other's company at the Gepps Cross Drive-In; snuggled together in Grant's 'Suburban' taxi.

Their courtship was brief and after only six weeks Grant asked her if she would like to spend the rest of her life with him. Nancy baulked at such an early proposal and told him, "I'll let you know tomorrow."

Grant spent a sleepless night hopeful his loved one would say yes. Early next morning, dressed in his Sunday best he knocked on the front door of the Ellis household. Nancy opened the door to find Grant beaming with excitement; he nervously showed her a deposit receipt from the Registrar's Office. He had them booked in to be married on the following Saturday morning! Nancy kissed Grant and gave an emphatic 'yes' to his proposal. On December 3, 1955 the marriage was celebrated with a reception at the Ambassador's Hotel on King William Street.

Jane Natarlie, their first-born, arrived on September 10, 1956. Like Arnna and Grant to follow, Jane was born in McBride

1 Grant and Nancy

Hospital, Medindie, near their first home in the inner city suburb of Joslin. Arnna Kathleen was born on November 1, 1958, and Grant Ellis on July 12, 1961.

Apart from the usual sickness and minor mishaps, perhaps the biggest drama the Beaumont parents had was when five-year-old Jane swallowed a hair clip.

Nancy: "I rushed her off to the doctors. And she had an X-ray. The hair clip was in her stomach right enough, but as the doctor said, it would take its own course."

The Beaumont parents and the doctor couldn't help but laugh when Jane saw the X-ray and wanted to put it in a frame and hang it on her bedroom wall.

Nancy was gradually dozing back off to sleep when Arnna and Grant startled her as they jumped on the bed. Jane soon joined the youngsters. The children were adamant today was going to be another fun day at the beach. During the summer holidays the children had practically lived on the Glenelg foreshore, mainly under the watchful eye of their father; Nancy didn't enjoy the beach as much as the rest of her family.

The children roared with approval when Nancy agreed to take them to Glenelg Beach as soon as all of her daily chores were completed. The children ran back to their rooms and quickly changed from their pyjamas into their bathing suits.

After breakfast the children became increasingly impatient; constantly questioning their mother, "Is it time yet?" They just couldn't wait.

In the end Nancy succumbed to the children's demands and allowed the three to travel to the beach without her; "As long as you are home by 12 o'clock." At first Nancy considered letting her children ride their bikes, but thought riding in the heat of the day would be too much for them and considered it would be safer for them to get on the bus at the corner of Diagonal Road than cross Brighton Road with their bikes during the busy morning peak-hour traffic.[9]

Nancy and Grant Beaumont were proud that they had installed into their children a measured degree of independence. Most Saturdays Jane and Arnna ventured down to the cinema at Glenelg by themselves; the two sisters had an extremely close relationship.

Jane and Arnna carried their paddle boards into the kitchen as they were about to depart but their mother told them to leave them at home. Nancy worried that her children might get into difficulties in the water, especially with little Grant with them.

Each child kissed their mother farewell at the front gate of their home. Nancy quietened the children down before she carefully explained the do's and don'ts of traveling to the beach without adult supervision. "Do not talk to any strangers, don't go into lonely places, and above all look after each other."

Little Grant chirped in: "Don't worry mummy. Well' be all right".

A neighbour from across the street shouted out to Nancy, "Where's your bikini Nancy?" Both of the women laughed.

Nancy: "Gosh I'd look lovely like that!"

Nancy Beaumont smiled with pride as she gazed at the delightful scene of her three children walking away from her, hand-in-hand along the street. "They turned around and waved to me. I went inside without a care in the world."

The time was 8.35 a.m.

1 Grant and Nancy

Nancy finished all of her housekeeping chores at 10 a.m. and decided to visit a friend. As she rode her bicycle down the side streets of Somerton she noticed how oppressively hot it had become so early in the day. She thought of her children and hoped they were sitting on the lawn in a shady spot.

At five minutes to midday Nancy was back on her bike heading for the bus stop on Diagonal Road so that she could meet the children and walk back home with them. The silver bus stopped but only an elderly woman alighted, so Nancy returned home and prepared lunch for herself.

Nancy was only home for a short while before friends dropped over unexpectedly. While she entertained her visitors Nancy kept an eye on the clock in the lounge room; the next available bus from Glenelg to Somerton Park was due to arrive around 2 p.m. At 2.15 p.m. Nancy became noticeably agitated as she waited for her children to come through the open front door.

Her friends offered to drive her down to Glenelg Beach to pick up the children but Nancy said it wouldn't be much help if the children had decided to walk home; there were a number of different routes they could have taken.

Nancy: "It's best if we wait for the three o'clock bus."

Just before 3 p.m. Nancy heard the familiar sound of the family car pull into the driveway. Grant had returned from his sales trip a day early. Nancy rushed outside to greet him.

"The kiddies haven't returned from the beach, I'm a little worried Grant."

Grant tried to calm her down. "Don't worry. They'll be all right. They'll be home. You would have heard if anything was wrong by now."

Grant Beaumont unhitched the caravan and drove directly to Glenelg. Outwardly he was composed to soothe his wife's fears; inside he was frantic.

Within minutes he was cruising down Jetty Road; his eyes darting in all directions looking for Jane, Arnna and little Grant. It was now 3.30 p.m. and the beach and surrounds were teaming with people seeking relief from the soaring temperature. He parked his car and walked to the area where he had last seen his children playing on the lawns at Colley Reserve. The area was packed with people but there was no sign of his children.

Grant's mouth became parched from his ever increasing anxiety. He ran onto the nearby jetty to get a better view of the beach but all he saw were thousands of people. He tried to quieten his mind and convinced himself that the children would surely be home by now. Driving home he envisioned walking through the front door and being greeted with hugs and smiles.

"I came back home again to see that I hadn't missed the children. But they still weren't home."

The distressed Beaumont parents returned to Glenelg Beach and began a second search. After two hours they realised their efforts were futile; the area was too large to cover without help so they walked to the Glenelg Police Station in Moseley Square and reported their three children missing. The time was 5 p.m.

Grant: "We saw the constable on duty at the desk. He rang up head office; I think. I waited there. He took a full description of what they were wearing and details of their ages. I don't know whom he rang in Adelaide. I wouldn't know police procedure. I went to the police station because it was the only thing to do. If you can't find you children you'd logically go to the police station."

1 Grant and Nancy

"They had never been missing from home before — I knew there was something wrong if they weren't home. The thought going through my mind was that they had been taken away. I didn't think they could have been drowned because there were so many people down there."

As the two distraught parents left the police station and walked towards their car, the temperature hit its peak of 102.3°F. The tarred, sticky pavement melted under their feet but Nancy and Grant were oblivious to the conditions; both were now numb with fear.

Driving down Harding Street both parents were silently praying for the same outcome; the children would be home waiting. As they walked through the front door they were greeted with silence.

A police car arrived soon after and two young officers searched the Beaumont home.

Nancy: "They searched the house because they felt perhaps the kiddies might be hiding. You know, these things have happened and the police are experienced at looking for people."

More senior officers then began questioning Nancy Beaumont about the time the children left home, what they were wearing and their physical descriptions.

When the police officers departed Grant left with them to help with the search.

Nancy: "My neighbour at the back stayed with me all night. To be honest, from there on I'm pretty vague. I think it just started to sink in then. Although I was walking around and talking, when I look back now it was just as if I looked through people."

"I wouldn't know just who was here."

That night, Nancy waited for the phone to ring with good

news, while Grant sat in the back seat of police patrol cars, cruising down every street in the Glenelg and Somerton area.

Grant: "I went out with the different patrol cars all night. I was either in them or walking along the beach at Seacliff, Brighton, Somerton, Glenelg, West Beach … right along."

"As I say, it was a hot night and everybody was lying on the beach. There were thousands still there at midnight. That didn't help matters."

"I didn't get to bed that night. The police dropped me back here early in the morning because it wouldn't be light until 4.30 a.m."

Grant Beaumont vowed that he would not go to bed until he had found his children.

"I got into my own car and I searched on my own along Brighton, Seacliff. I don't know how long I searched. All I was intent on doing was to keep on searching."

2

"It's all my fault"

January 27, 1966

At 7.00 a.m. Grant Beaumont drove into his driveway, exhausted after a futile search. He dreaded walking into his childless home however he was desperately worried about his wife, now being cared for by neighbours and relatives.

Grant found Nancy slumped in a lounge chair in the company of her mother. Her eyes were red raw from constant weeping. She couldn't even look at Grant she was so distraught and kept admonishing herself, "It's all my fault. I should never have let them go." The family doctor arrived shortly after and administered Nancy with a strong sedative.

Dozens of South Australian Police officers spent the night searching along the beaches' of Somerton, Brighton, and Glenelg. Five boats from the Sea Rescue Squadron had set out at 5 a.m. and searched the shoreline from Glenelg all the way south to Aldinga and back to Henley Beach, checking hollows and looking for evidence of cave-ins.

Detectives both at Glenelg and at Police Headquarters in the CBD of Adelaide, worked through the night trying to string together the known facts and a possible time-line into the children's disappearance.

Mid morning, an exhausted and distraught Grant met with the media who were eagerly waiting on the back porch of the Beaumont's home. He pleaded for his children to be returned: "Somebody must be holding them against their will. They would otherwise have come home by now."

Grant and the police had already ruled out the only other two options for their disappearance; either the children had runaway or they had drowned. He knew the children had no motive to go into hiding and the chance of all three children drowning amongst thousands of beach goers was near impossible. Besides, no articles of clothing, towels or the bag belonging to the children had been located. In his mind, the only plausible scenario was that his children had been abducted.

Grant: "It's a complete mystery. I can't understand it. My kids will be crying their eyes out. It is like a nightmare."

With blackened eyes through lack of sleep, he repeated his frustration, "It's the waiting around, the suspense. I don't know where to go, where to look."

"It's hard to say what happened. If Jane was told to be home by 2 o'clock she'd be home by 2 o'clock. They never would have gone with a stranger."

He told the reporters his children knew their way home from

"anywhere around here," and had made a similar trip home from Glenelg Beach only the day before.

Grant: "Jane's only nine, but she's got the brain of a girl of 15. We'd never have let them go otherwise. She's corrected me when I've taken a wrong street in the car, and sometimes I do it deliberately."

Mr Beaumont speculated that his three children would have walked through Moseley Square. "There was usually a crowd at that part of the beach, lifesavers were nearby and they could have looked at the side-shows if they had been open."

The impromptu media conference ended when Grant Beaumont bowed his head and began to weep.

The police issued detailed descriptions of the children hoping someone would come forward with information to shed light on this tragic mystery.

Jane Nartalie Beaumont — aged 9, 4 ft. 6 in. (137cm) tall, thin build, sun bleached, ear-length fair hair pushed back with fringe in front, possibly wearing tortoise shell hair band with yellow ribbon, hazel eyes and thin, freckled face with two prominent front teeth. She wore green shorts over pink bathers, canvas tartan sandshoes with white soles. She could have been carrying the book 'Little Women'. She could also have an airways-type shoulder bag and three towels. She had a white money purse containing 8-6 (85c). Well spoken but stutters when excited.

Arnna Kathleen Beaumont — aged 7, 4ft (122cm) tall, plump build, dark brown hair with fringe, sun-tanned complexion, dark brown eyes. She wore tan shorts over red and white striped bathers and tan sandals.

Grant Ellis Beaumont — aged 4, 3 ft. (91cm) tall, thin build, brown hair with fringe, brown eyes, olive complexion, sun tanned, was wearing green swim trunks, with vertical white stripes under green cotton shorts and red sandals. He was not wearing a shirt.

All through the day police cars fitted with loudspeaker's toured the Glenelg streets appealing for help from the public. "Has anyone seen three small children … please contact police immediately?"

Shocked relatives and friends gathered at the Beaumont family home trying to comfort the distraught parents as they waited for news. A phone was installed so they could be in constant contact with Glenelg CIB.

The Glenelg shopping precinct became a hive of activity. People flocked to Moseley Square to show support for the Beaumont parents and to lend a helping hand in the search.

The Glenelg Police Station, situated in the heart of Moseley Square was inundated with people claiming to have found a 'clue'. Dozens of rubber thongs, shoes and scraps of old clothing were brought to the station's front desk. The limited number of police personnel at the station were being stretched to their limits; numbers were soon doubled to cope with the influx of 'information' from the public.

The front desk of the Glenelg police station was tiny and grossly inadequate for the unfolding drama, as it also served as the witness waiting room for courthouse proceedings. In the early stages of the investigation, people were lined up for over twenty metres onto Moseley Square, waiting to make a statement to police. Each statement from the public had to be

2 "It's all my fault"

recorded on the one available typewriter. The influx of information soon became chaotic to organise.

Dozens of taxi drivers roamed the streets looking for signs of the missing children. The manager of Suburban Taxis, Mr W Lay, told reporters Grant Beaumont had been an owner driver with his company for many years. "As soon as the boys heard that it was Jimmy's children who were missing, they came to me and asked that I ring the police and seek permission for them to join in the search. Jimmy is a likeable chap, and was very popular with the drivers when he was with us."

Men, women and children joined squads of police as they combed the sand-hills and shacks north of Glenelg. Disused premises were thoroughly searched as were cinemas, golf links, the Morphettville Race Course, and vacant allotments. Nothing was uncovered.

Police also put into place heavy surveillance at the Adelaide Airport, and Adelaide Railway Station and set up road blocks on all highways to ensure that the abductor could not escape the State.

Girls of the Third Somerton Brownie Pack, of which Jane Beaumont was a member, rode in 'single file' around the suburban streets hoping to find their lost friend.

The community of Adelaide was in shock. The unthinkable crime drew out the best in its citizens. However shock soon turned to fear.

"They were holding hands and laughing..."

Within 24 hours of their disappearance, S.A. Homicide detectives released details of what they believed to be the last known movements of the Beaumont children. According to driver, Mr I D Munro, the children had boarded his bus, (operated by the company, R Worthley and Sons) at the corner of Harding Street and Diagonal Road soon after 10 a.m. on Wednesday. He remembered seeing the children entering the bus, but he could not remember where they alighted. "I definitely remember picking up three children at the Harding Street stop at about 10.10 a.m." However Munro said he could not remember the same three children returning on any of the buses he drove out of Glenelg in the afternoon.

The children's bus route travelled along Diagonal Road, Brighton and Jetty Roads and then took a left turn into Moseley Street, the bus' terminus. According to Grant Beaumont, "The children were familiar with the journey but on the rare occasion that they overran the home stop they would walk back."

The last confirmed sighting was from postman, Tom Patterson, who was known to the Beaumont family. Patterson spotted the children in the afternoon as they walked along Jetty Road, about to cross over to Moseley Street, "They were holding hands and laughing." He heard one of the children say, "Hey there's our postie".

Patterson contacted police on the night of the disappearance but was somewhat vague of the exact time of his sighting. He was unsure whether he saw the children as he began his afternoon postal round at around at 1.45 p.m., or when he had finished his deliveries at 2.55 p.m.

Patterson spent a sleepless night mulling over the day's events and on the Thursday morning he told police, "I remember now that I forgot to deliver a parcel a few minutes before I saw the children, and this was at the end of my round. The more I think it must have seen them just before 3 o'clock."

Wanda Murders

The disappearance of the Beaumont children occurred just one year after the murder of two children at Wanda Beach, Sydney, causing speculation about a possible connection amongst the media.

Marianne Schmidt and Christine Sharrock, both 15, were murdered on January 11, 1965. That morning the two girls, and Marianne's four siblings, set off for Cronulla (approximately 25 km south of Sydney's CBD). They arrived at around 11 a.m., but the beach was closed because of gale-force winds. The children walked to the southern end of the beach and sheltered from the stinging sand, amongst the rocks. Marianne told her younger siblings that she and Christine were going back to retrieve the bags they had left behind. They never returned. Their partially buried bodies were discovered the next day. They had been raped and mutilated with a knife.

S.A. Police issued a statement regarding a possible link between the Beaumont children's disappearance and the Wanda Beach murders. "It is a possibility and we are not ruling it out".

An Elderly Witness

January 29 — The first breakthrough in the investigation came when a 74-year-old Glenelg woman came forward and claimed she saw the Beaumont children "frolicking" with a man on the lawn beside the Holdfast Bay Sailing Club (Colley Reserve), at around 11 a.m. on January 26th. The woman's report led to a state-wide search for a tall, thin, blond haired man in his thirties; a "sun-baked swimmer." Some media outlets described the man as a "middle aged surfie"; or as having an "unruly mop of blonde bleached hair."

The woman remembered the elder girl wearing pink bathers, the same colour as Jane Beaumont wore under her shorts when she and her siblings left home. She claimed the children carried an 'airways' bag similar to the one the Beaumont children had taken to the beach.

She related to police how she was sitting on a wooden bench near the Holdfast Bay Sailing Club when she saw two girls and a boy come up from the sea after a swim. They laid out their towels in the shade of a secluded corner of the foreshore hidden by the sailing club and the back of the sideshows and began playing under a sprinkler.

Her attention then focused on a tall blonde-haired man who began talking to the children. The man also lay on a towel on the lawn area about 10 ft. from her. He wore brief navy blue bathers.

According to the woman, the three children went over to the man. The boy jumped over him, the younger girl followed suite; the older girl playfully began flicking the man with a towel. "He was laughing and encouraging them as they played."

Half an hour later when the woman got up to walk home, the man and the children were still playing together on the lawn.

Detective Blight, the head of the Glenelg CIB, questioned the woman and concluded that the children she described were definitely the Beaumont children; "Almost beyond doubt."

Piecing together a time-line of the children's movements was proving to be difficult. The Beaumont family's postman, Tom Patterson, returned to the Glenelg Police Station two days after his initial statement and told detectives that on further reflection he thought it had been on Wednesday morning, and not on the Wednesday afternoon that he had seen the children. This was not the only piece of information regarding the time line which was to be challenged.

All media outlets across Australia had reported that the children took the 10.10 a.m. bus from Somerton Park to Glenelg; even though Nancy Beaumont confirmed in a later interview that the children caught the 8.45 a.m. bus.

A Darlington man phoned *The News* suggesting he had evidence the children had left for Glenelg an hour earlier than what had been published.

He said his wife had seen the children on the bus and was positive of the time. "She could not have made a mistake, because it was her first day at work and she reached Glenelg about 8.55 a.m." The caller said his wife was certain the children were the Beaumonts.

"She is a 'cub mistress' and not likely to make mistakes about children."

The witness had remembered the children because she was surprised when they got onto the bus alone. The two younger children stood only a few feet in front of her; the older one walked to the rear of the bus and started to read a book.

The woman said that during the bus trip the older girl had chided the little boy for putting his arm out the window. "He went to put his arm out again but stopped and turned around and cheekily smiled at her."

The search for the children quickly became Australia wide. Sydney police were put on alert after a report the children were seen on board a Sydney-bound plane that departed Adelaide 24 hours after the abduction. A man traveling on the plane said he saw a blonde "surfie" sitting near three children resembling the Beaumonts. He told police the surfie appeared agitated.

In Western Australia, detectives at Merredin, about 200 miles east of Perth, questioned a hitch-hiker who resembled the wanted 'surfie' man.

Tasmanian police started a full-scale search for a mystery stranger seen in Hobart fitting the description of the man wanted by Adelaide detectives. He was described as 6 ft. 1 in. slim build, deeply tanned in his late 30s, and with long unkempt sun-bleached hair. Most of the reports centred on the Sandy Bay area. He had been heard talking to a small boy about Adelaide.

Police received hundreds of calls in the first 48 hours of the abduction from people who believed they had seen the three missing children.

There was a report from a woman who saw three children, in the company of two men in a bus at Semaphore Park on the Wednesday afternoon.

A woman living in the suburb of Malvern told police that on the night of the disappearance, she saw a man and three children enter a supposedly vacant house opposite her home. She claimed that at one point, a little boy had walked down a side lane, but the man had come out, grabbed him and pulled him back inside. There was no sign of the man or the children the following day.

Other 'sightings' of the suntanned swimmer were recorded at Norwood Parade, the Adelaide Railway Station, in a car on Main North Road, Nailsworth, in the Port Noarlunga sand hills, a home in Brighton, and a Glenelg café.

Police were also alerted to the fact that a number of Glenelg residents believed they had seen a 'tall blonde man' at the beach in the days leading up to January 26. The man was seen "lurking around" during the day in the empty sideshow allies as well as around the sailing club, "Watching children on the beach."

Detective-Sergeant A. Palmer, the head of the Adelaide CIB Homicide Squad, summarised the tragic event that was gripping the nation, "At the moment we see a picture of a man striking up a conversation with the children. Arnna, the seven-year-old girl would approach anyone and held no fear. Arnna could have frolicked round the man with her brother Grant. When Jane, the quiet, sensible one, had her confidence bolstered, she may have joined in. It is feasible that the children would have accepted an invitation because they had spent all their money on ice-creams and drinks."

"At this time or some time later, he could have offered to take them home. From then on, we are in the dark."

Police detectives involved with the case were completely baffled and pessimistic on their prospects of solving the mystery. Only two days after the disappearance an unnamed detective told a local newspaper, "Nothing... absolutely nothing clicks into place and unless we get a new lead it's going to be hard to break."

The 'Pat'

The Patawalonga Boat Haven was drained three days after the disappearance when a woman reported to police she had spoken to three children, similar in description to the Beaumont children at the Boat Haven at about 7 p.m. on Wednesday, January 26.

The woman saw two girls and a young boy at the water's edge below the southern side of the old Patawalonga Bridge. She approached the children and asked them for directions to Mary Street, Glenelg North (a few streets from the bridge), but the children said they did not live in the area.

Police took no chances and immediately put into place a plan to search the boat haven once the water had been drained.

Crowds of spectators watched police aqualung divers searching the boat haven but the visibility in the murky water was almost non-existent.

The locked gates of the Patawalonga basin were opened from the lock near the Glenelg migrant hostel. It was the first time the haven had been emptied since it was built in 1959.

The haven covered an area of 70 acres and is normally filled to a depth of 6 feet. A party of police cadets from the Fort Largs Police Academy stood nearby ready to begin a search.

Former police officer, Max Slee recalled the search of the 'Pat' as a cadet. Slee was only a teenager like the other 80 or so cadets (some were as young as sixteen) who were loaded into buses at the Fort Largs Police Academy. "We were all in our khaki pants and top — sports shoes ... it was stinking hot and no-one had a hat. On the way to Glenelg an academy instructor stopped the bus at a hardware store and summoned six or so boys to follow him. Inside the large store, the instructor immediately asked to see the manager. 'It's urgent'. When the manager appeared from his office the instructor asked 'How many broom handle have you in stock? I'll take the lot'. Before long the cadets were loading dozens of wooden poles into the bus. None of us had any idea what they were for."

The broom handles were used as prodding sticks in the thick black mud of the drained 'Pat'. Some of the boys stripped down to their underwear as they slowly walked in a grid pattern to search for anything regarding the lost children. The putrid black mud stank as the cadets slowly sank into it. Nothing pertaining to the lost children was uncovered.

Journalists, photographers and film crews from around Australia congregated at Glenelg eager to capture the moment a breakthrough in this mystery occurred. Any police officer sighted walking the streets of Glenelg were accosted for an 'interview'. In the early days of the disappearance there were approximately 100 reporters in the Glenelg shopping precinct hoping for an 'exclusive' such was the interest in this case.

Local media personality Kevin Crease was one of the first journalists on the scene when the children were first reported missing. He planned to keep one step ahead of the ever growing media pack.

For 10 days after the children's disappearance, Crease (at the time an ABC TV journalist), was stationed only metres from the front door of the Glenelg Police Station in an outside broadcast van. At night, he and his capable cameraman, Dean Semler (later to win an Oscar for cinematography in the film, Dances With Wolves) were bunked up on the 2nd level of the old Pier Hotel which overlooked the police station.

"We were there for about a week, taking it in turns to sleep; the other one would keep an eye on what was going on and if anything looked interesting, we'd wake the other one up and jump in our car and take off after the police. Eventually it got to the ridiculous stage where we'd follow them if they were going down to get a hamburger or something. They'd say to us 'For God's sake, will you leave us alone'."

"Attractive Witness"

An "attractive 19-year-old girl" became the next major witness to come forward. *The News* reported that police detectives had received vital information on the possible movements of the "blonde beachcomber".

The woman said she had seen a man fitting the description issued by police, playing with two girls and a boy.

"I can remember the man well — he was lying facing me. Nearly all the time I was there he was staring at me."

"He kept glancing at the three children running around him on the beach."

She told the police the man had been lying on a towel on the beach just north of the Pier Hotel.

"I went down to the beach just before noon and was only 50 ft. from him. He kept staring at me. Then, between noon and 12.20 p.m., the children walked in front of me. They were laughing and playing."

The young woman was watching the children play, when the older girl shouted at her. "Are you trying to con, or catch my brother?"

"I ignored the girl, but noticed the man had been attracted by the girl's remark".

She then saw the children walk in a southerly direction towards Somerton with the man following them; but he returned a short time later with a woman.

"They [man and woman] walked towards the Holdfast Bay Sailing Club. The woman looked to be about 35, medium height, with brown curly hair. She was wearing a bone-coloured shift".

"...Two best witnesses"

On February 2nd, two more witnesses contacted police. Detective Blight described the elderly couple — as the "two best witnesses" yet to come forward. The witnesses told police they saw a man with the Beaumont children on the foreshore lawns on the day the children disappeared. They described the man and the children as being "very friendly" and that he "dressed" the children, putting their shorts on over their bathers before walking away with his own clothes towards the change rooms at Colley Reserve.

Their information had confirmed the description of the man given by four other people who said they had seen the man with the children on the lawns on the same day.

Police said the couple were sitting on a bench with their grand-daughter. Shortly before noon they noticed the man and the children on the lawn behind the seat where another witness (the 74-year-old woman) had been sitting.

Just after midday, the man approached the couple and asked, "Did any of you people see anyone with our clothes?"

When they asked why, he said "We've had some money taken from our clothes."

The couple explained that they had only just arrived, and hadn't seen anything untoward. The man returned to the children. A short while later the woman had her curiosity aroused, when she witnessed the man dress the children. She thought it was strange, especially as the elder girl appeared to be old enough to dress herself. She then witnessed the man who wore brief dark blue bathers, pick up his towel and a pair of trousers and walk north along a pathway towards the changing shed. The children waited outside the shed.

The Artist

The News organised for its in-house artist Peter von Czarnecki to help police put together a sketch from the descriptions the witnesses had given to police.

Von Czarnecki was taken to Glenelg for an interview with the woman. The woman could only provide a limited description of the man's features; she could not recall the shape or the colour of his eyes nor the shape of his mouth and nose. The limited amount of specific detail was obvious when the artist's final drawing was revealed.

The image of the man wanted by police could only be described as a 'general idea' of the suspect although later that night a second person confirmed the sketch resembled the man wanted for questioning.

"Today is world of prayer..."

The Beaumont parents were engulfed with pain at their loss.

Newspaper men were camped outside their home almost 24 hours a day. Grant wanted action and did not hesitate to use the press to get his message across. He appeared on television just over 48 hours after the children were reported missing and pleaded with the abductor of his children.

"Today is world of prayer throughout Australia for Australia Day. I hope whoever is holding my children will return them. Please if anyone knows anything about my children, in God's name, act quickly… If I had won the lottery I could understand it, and would be willing to pay a ransom, but I am just a salesman, and nobody has approached us."

"It is hard to believe that three small children could continue roaming the streets without being observed."

Arrested Three Times

South Australian's were on full alert. Anyone vaguely resembling the 'suntanned swimmer' was looked upon with suspicion.

A man with a striking resemblance to the 'suspect' was arrested three times in just five days!

The man was at Adelaide Airport when he noticed people staring at him and taking down details of his car when he drove away from the airport. He realised what was happening, and drove straight to Police HQ and "gave himself up". His name was soon cleared of suspicion. Later in the week the man, who lived in Glenelg, was detained at the Glenelg Police Station and was grilled for hours by detectives such was his resemblance to the 'blonde surfie'.

His third apprehension came while he was in the city near the Adelaide Railway Station. A member of the public saw him and telephoned police. Several police patrols sped to the North Terrace destination and once again detained him before his inevitable release.

A terrible silence

Weary detectives who had been on the case almost night and day since the disappearance started to confide to journalists the enormity and the hopelessness of the investigation. One detective put it bluntly, "The common denominator has been nothing. Where do we go now?"

Another detective was quoted as saying, "Anything factual about them [the Beaumont children] came to a shuddering halt at 11.30 a.m. on Wednesday, January 26. Try as we may, we cannot find one lead which gives us a solid clue to their whereabouts beyond that time. Anything could have happened to them since."

Detectives had been checking on every known sexual pervert on their books, seeking out men who may fit the description of the man seen with the children, however every one of them seemed to have a solid alibi.

According to Superintendent Lenton, Chief of the CIB, the public response had been "magnificent." In an incredible statistic, he reported that over 1,000 supposed 'sightings' had been reported to police in only the first seven days of the investigation.

"We have had hundreds of letters suggesting new angles, and all have been checked. Nothing is being excluded, even though many letters come from people claiming to be clairvoyants, diviners, or dreamers."

Rumours started spreading like wild-fire in the city of Adelaide. On February 4th there had been no less than four different 'confirmed' stories doing the rounds. 'The children had been found' in four different cities: Sydney, Melbourne, Broken Hill, and then Renmark. All were false.

After six days of mental torture, Nancy Beaumont received the all clear from her doctor to face questioning from the press. The previous night was the first time she had eaten for days. Numb from heavy sedative medication, she pleaded for the return of her children.

"I love my children. Please let me have them back."

Nancy sat on a wooden bench and lent on the round picnic table in the secluded backyard of their family home. Her husband sat beside her with a comforting arm around her waist.

"I can't be stupid, and say they're going to come in with a skipping rope."

"I've got to feel that the little things are huddled up somewhere and nobody has found them."

Nancy Beaumont leant on her husband's shoulder as tears rolled down her cheek. The men and women of the media dropped their heads and stared at the ground whilst Nancy gained composure.

"Excuse me for crying in front of you fellows. I've got to keep busy. I do little jobs, mop floors, clean ashtrays and smoke cigarettes."

"I've done my little share of praying all to myself."

Grant Beaumont handed around to the reporters a letter from their eldest daughter Jane. She had written the letter only two nights before the tragedy. Grant wanted to show the world how caring and mature Jane was as she had 'baby-sat' Arnna and Grant during her parents' brief absence that night.

"Dear Mum and Dad, I am just about to go to bed and the time is 9. I have put Grant's nappy on so there is no need to worry about him wetting on the sheet. Grant wanted to sleep in his

own bed so one of you will have to sleep with Arnna. Although you will not find the rooms in very good condition I hope you will find them as comfortable as we do. Good night to you both.

Jane.

PS I hope you had a very nice time wherever you went.

PPS I hope you don't mind me taking your radio into my room Daddy."

Nancy Beaumont: "I was going to show it to her when she grew up and tell her what a beautiful girl she was".

"They're very affectionate — they're lovely to one another".

"If the other two were very keen to be with somebody, Jane would go with them to look after them and wouldn't leave them alone."

Nancy looked puzzled, "I cannot understand why Jane, a shy girl, much more so than Arnna and Grant, would allow a man to put her shorts on, even over her bathers … people who have told police that they saw a man and three children at Glenelg say she did."

Nancy stared into space and kept shaking her head, perplexed with disbelief.

"I'm inclined to think it was all over on the Wednesday afternoon. Whoever it was had nothing to lose. These thoughts have been with me for a long while — not since yesterday, but since Thursday last week. I'm looking at both sides, but I don't know what to think any more".

One of the reporters listening to Nancy and Grant was Victorian journalist Tom Prior who was representing *The Herald* newspaper. Grant and Tom immediately struck up a good rapport and would become long time friends.

2 "It's all my fault"

After the media pack had left the Beaumont home Grant and Tom walked to the Glenelg Police Station to talk to the detectives in charge of the investigation. Since his children went missing, every morning and afternoon, Grant would walk the three kilometres to ask the same question: "Any news?"

Glenelg CIB detectives were welcoming to Grant but their sombre faces told a story of despondency. On the wall behind the Sergeant's front desk there was a cork pin-board with mug shots of men; all were known sexual predators in the area, unfortunately all could explain their whereabouts on January 26th.

The police officers knew what Grant's first question would be, and were frustrated with the only answer they could give.

"Nothing new, but honestly, Mr Beaumont we're trying…"

Grant: "I know you are; I know you are. And don't think the wife and I don't appreciate it. But it's been six days now — five nights — and they're only little kids."

Grant stood up from his chair and paced up and down Sergeant Ron 'Wingy' Blight's office.

"Grant is only four and he'd get frightened at night. He still wears nappies at night. Who could keep a little boy like that away from his mother? Jane is a very sensible kid; she'd look after the little ones as long as she could … but its six days now."

Grant's voice began to break with pent-up emotion.

A detective told him, "We're getting new leads all the time, Mr Beaumont. We'll find them."

Grant: "But they must be so frightened. I'm not a religious man, but the only thing I can do now is pray. A lot of people are praying for us."

As Grant stood up to leave the station, the head of the Glenelg CIB, Detective Ron Blight, put his arm on his shoulder and escorted the emotional father to the front door.

Blight felt the pain of Beaumont acutely. He was the same age as Grant and eerily had three children with the exact same ages as those missing.

Blight was an experienced cop having worked for many years at Port Adelaide CIB, Adelaide CIB's Vice Squad, Breaking Squad and Safe Squad, but this was by far the "worst case of all." He and his colleagues Moss Matters and Lloyd Brand had worked over 150 hours (non paid) overtime between them in the first week of the case. He took the lack of a break-through personally. "No matter how long one has been in the Police Force, no matter what one has seen, one can never get used to things like this."

As the tormented parent and journalist left the station, Grant handed Tom a photograph of his children. Grant wanted the photograph to be shown in Victoria where most of his army mates were located.

Grant, "It's a good photograph. And maybe someone will see it and recognise the kids. You can see Jane's teeth are a little prominent in the front and the fringe of hair on Grant's forehead."

"And that's Arnna to a T, with the big grin. It's my favourite photo. We took it on a country trip in October and, well, we were all happy then…"

Walking back to his home, Grant revealed to Prior that he was certain his children were alive; he insisted they were probably being held in a hut in a remote country area by a "kindly eccentric".

Back at the Harding Street home, Nancy told Prior. "My

children are dead and I know it. I mustn't think they are, but I can't be stupid. It's just been too long I don't think they're alive."

Grant reached over to comfort her but Nancy shook her head.

Nancy: "The poor little things are huddled up somewhere in some stupid place and the police will never find them. I haven't given up hope, but I know."

"The children all loved one another, and they'd have stuck together. If one was hurt, the others would have chipped in. That's why they all died together; they wouldn't have run off in different directions."

"I've said prayers. I want my children to come back. I don't want anything else. All the things you thought were important don't matter. Even our home is incidental now. I'd rather we were all together in a tent on the beach."

Nancy was obviously feeling the devastation of her loss as well as being influenced by the affect of prescription drugs.

"I'm numb. I can't feel my stomach and I can't feel my head. I don't know what is happening. I just know that our Janie was a lovely girl, modest and kind, and a wonderful daughter. Arnna was a loveable little thinker, and so beautiful. Grant was our son, only four-years-old, and now they're dead, I know it…"

"I think as a mother, I'd rather kill the children myself and get it over quickly than have them at the mercy of some bad person for so long."

3

The Man With the Crazy Walk

Monday, February 7 was the first day of the new school year for thousands of South Australian children and another heart-breaking hurdle for Grant and Nancy to overcome. In the past, the start of the school year had brought happiness to the Beaumont home. 'Back to school' had been an exciting time for the children as they were always eager to catch up with their many friends. For Grant it was another opportunity to take photos of his precious family. Grant caught the 'photo bug' when he purchased his first camera while stationed in Japan and had a cupboard full of photo albums, mainly of his family on their many caravanning adventures.

But today Grant knew that the further away from the family home the better it was going to be for the wellbeing of himself and his wife. He was acutely aware that the sight of students from Paringa Park Primary School would be too traumatic for

Nancy. Along with two friends they drove down to Christie's Beach for a picnic. The time away was comforting for the Beaumont parents, but when they returned, late in the afternoon they were once again greeted with the pain of reality.

Waiting for them was reporter Ted Harrison from *The News*.

The Beaumonts were always welcoming and gracious towards journalists; they believed that any publicity might hold the key to bringing an end to their nightmare.

Harrison was shown the rooms of the children which had been left untouched for 13 days. Jane and Arnna's straw school hats with green and gold ribbons hung on metal hooks in the passage way; dolls and toys lay neatly at the end of the children's beds.

It was a warm night and Grant took Harrison out the back door to get some fresh air. Harrison could not help but notice the children's belongings scattered around the yard. He recorded: "An empty swing swung silently in the breeze as Grant Beaumont stared at the new bicycle Arnna, would have ridden to school today. It was hidden from Mrs Beaumont vision in the garage, Arnna got it for Christmas."

Grant pointed to a freshly painted red go-kart which had a small plastic container dangling from the steering wheel. Grant explained to Harrison how he had added the container so his son could put sixpences and threepence's in it and make believe he was a taxi driver.

Grant: "It's his taxi — just like Dad's. I used to have two taxis myself." "I still think they will come through the gate one day. They would have to, wouldn't they?"

'Gunner' Kelly

There were mixed feelings amongst the S.A. Police hierarchy when a recently retired, high ranking N.S.W. Police officer arrived in Adelaide with a fanfare of media attention. Former detective Ray Kelly was hired by *The Sun* newspaper to report on the investigation into the missing children which was quickly turning cold.

Kelly had been a decorated but controversial figure in his long career fighting crime in Sydney.

Nicknamed "Machine Gun", "Gunner" or "Verbal", Kelly gained national fame as the head of the investigation into the notorious kidnapping and murder of Sydney schoolboy Graeme Thorne, aged 8, in 1960. The boy's father, Bazil Thorne became the winner of an Opera House Lottery, which was set up to fund the construction of the harbour city's iconic landmark. Not only were the delighted faces of Thorne and his family featured in all of the newspapers, their home address was also published.

Hungarian migrant factory worker, Stephen Leslie Bradley, (34) saw an opportunity and laid a plan to kidnap the boy.

Bradley waited in his 1955 blue Ford for Graeme Thorne, at the spot where the boy was usually dropped off at school. Bradley enticed the boy into his car and drove to a secluded area in Centennial Park, where he tied a scarf around Graeme's mouth and locked him in the boot of the car.

Bradley then rang the Thorne home demanding a ransom. "I want 25,000 pounds by five o'clock this afternoon or I'll feed him to the sharks."

3 The Man With the Crazy Walk

A number of hours later when Bradley unlocked the boot of his car, the poor boy was barely alive. The kidnapper panicked and strangled Graeme Thorne before dumping the body in a nearby paddock.

Bradley was eventually tracked down and sentenced to life imprisonment due to the brilliant detective work headed by Ray Kelly.

Kelly gained further credence only days before he retired. He captured notorious prison escapees Ronald Ryan (the last person to be legally executed in Australia) and Peter John Walker in January 1966. However, there has since been speculation that crime boss Lenny McPherson, may have been involved. It has been alleged that McPherson set up a bogus meeting with Walker and Ryan at Concord Hospital in Sydney and tipped off Kelly.

Kelly also became legendary for his prowess in 'coercing' confessions from criminals. He became so effective at this practice, Sydney barrister Simon Isaacs nicknamed him "Verbal Kelly".

On his arrival in Adelaide, Kelly made an unofficial visit to police headquarters to visit the Chief of the CIB, Superintendent Noel Lenton; a close friend. Later that night he dined at the Ambassadors Hotel, in King William Street with several senior police officers. The cordial welcome from the heads of the S.A. Police was short lived.

The following day Kelly surprised and somewhat embarrassed S.A. Police by claiming to have found a new person of interest in the children's disappearance. While door-knocking the Somerton Park area, he uncovered a prospective witness. Miss Daphne Gregory, who helped run a stable of horses in the area, described a man who had "averted his gaze" as he walked with three children along Boundary Road, Somerton Park shortly before 3 p.m. on Wednesday, January 26.

She gave a particularly detailed description of the man. "About 6 ft., aged from 30 to 35, carrying a dark airline-type bag (similar to one the Beaumont children had when they left home); walked with a slight swagger ("swinging arms, bowed at the elbows"); light brown hair; sun-reddened complexion, high cheek bones."

The woman told Kelly that at about 2.45 p.m. on January 26, she had been waiting in her car near her horse stables at the intersection of Boundary and Brighton Roads, Somerton Park, within a few hundred yards of the Beaumont house.

She had been on the lookout out for children as she suspected some had thrown sand into the back of her car earlier that day.

About 3 p.m. she noticed a tall man walking along Boundary Road towards Brighton with three children. He wore a light shirt and dark trousers. She had particularly noticed a slight swagger in his gait, suggesting that he was "muscle-bound".

The two girls and boy were wearing shorts over their bathers. The older girl wore "something reddish pink." The little boy looked tired and lagged behind.

Kelly believed the Boundary Road sighting was significant because it tallied with what neighbours of the Beaumonts had told him. It was claimed that the missing children normally walked along Boundary Road on the way to their home.

Earlier in the day Kelly talked to Tom Patterson, the postman. Patterson back-flipped once more; he now believed he had seen the three children shortly before 3 p.m. and not in the

3 The Man With the Crazy Walk

morning as he had earlier told police. He did confirm to Kelly the children were definitely alone.

Glenelg CIB detectives replied to Kelly's 'new' revelations via the media with a diplomatic statement saying that they appreciated Kelly's interest in the case but they believed the strongest lead was still the tall 'surfie' man, seen frolicking with three children on the lawn at Colley Reserve, Glenelg. The police emphasised that the man in question had still not come forward to clear his name.

Kelly countered this argument by declaring that the group (man and three children) seen at Colley Reserve may have been members of an interstate family that had returned home after a beach holiday in Adelaide. He said this theory was supported by the fact that this 'surfie' man approached an elderly couple sitting on a bench on the Glenelg foreshore and asked them: "Have you seen anybody messing around with our clothes? Our money has been pinched."

Kelly reasoned that a person intending to abduct children, would not want to draw attention to himself with such an approach.

The following day Ray Kelly organised a widespread hunt for "the man with the crazy walk."

"I feel very strongly that this is the man who took the missing Beaumont children. I am almost certain of it."

Police hit back

Ray Kelly surprisingly cut short his investigation into the Beaumont case because of what one newspaper described as "sensationalistic publicity". Apparently statements attributed to

Kelly in a Sydney newspaper had angered Adelaide detectives so much that CIB Chief Lenton issued a statement hotly denying the allegations.

"*The Sun* which engaged Kelly as a private investigator turned his genuine efforts to solve the case into a circus. Some stories, with little basis or foundation, were published without Kelly's knowledge or consent."

It was clear the headlines regarding Kelly's investigations; 'new leads', 'fresh clues' and 'early breakthroughs' put the local detectives' collective noses out of joint.

A weekend story in the *Sun-Herald* was the last straw. It claimed Kelly "had advanced the search more in two days in Adelaide than the local police had done in 15 days."

Another allegation claimed that most Adelaide detectives on the case were off duty on the weekend, and "one of the key investigators was taking the whole of this week off."

Lenton stood up for his men and declared that Kelly had apparently ignored organisation principles. "We have had a small team of detectives from Glenelg co-ordinating this search. They have worked to the limits of physical endurance trying to arrive at a solution to this case."

Lenton: "South Australian Police have done everything humanly possible to solve the mystery… Kelly had not produced one single new lead in the private inquiry."

Whilst Kelly and SA Police were fighting, a nine-year-old Paringa Park school girl came forward and told detectives she had seen the Beaumont children at Glenelg about 10 a.m. on January 26 and further interviews with the children's friends at Paringa Park

Primary School convinced detectives that the three children seen on the lawns were definitely the missing Beaumonts.

After three torturous weeks coping with the disappearance of his children, Grant Beaumont decided it was time to return to his career as a traveling salesman accompanied by Nancy. Even though the company he worked for had kept him on the payroll, Grant was adamant he had to return to some form of normality. Family, friends, neighbours and complete strangers had provided an assortment of gifts and services to the Beaumonts, but Grant told a friend "I don't want to live on charity."

The grieving parents had spent a week having time-out at a secluded fishing town, trying to come to terms with their horrendous loss.

Grant: "I was just beginning to get everything right — a nice little home, three lovely children. It looks as though I will have to sell the house to get by. I don't know how long this waiting is going to last."

Grant Beaumont revealed how worried he was for Nancy's mental health. For over two weeks he had been trying desperately to get Nancy away from the family home where memories haunted her however Nancy was now finding it difficult to leave their hideaway.

Grant: "Now she is here away from the things that reminded her every moment of the children, she doesn't want to leave. I don't know where we go from here."

Nancy: "My children had all they wanted in the world. All they want is their mother and father … and all we want is the children. The house could fall down around our ears, and we wouldn't worry. Money means nothing to us — only the happiness of the children."

Nancy's eyes softened for a moment when she started to speak of Jane who she described as a "wonderful little mother" to the other two children.

Nancy: "She topped her class in Grade III the year before last and last year came second by only half a mark. I never have to ask her to help with the dishes because she always offers before I can even think about it. She cleans out her own room. She keeps it so tidy it's almost like a little department store with everything in its right place."

"But she's shy — much shier than the other two. That's why I can't understand anybody being able to lure her away."

"Arnna is the little actress of the family; a real personality … a little singer. She wanders around the back garden…"

Grant Beaumont talked of his namesake who he said often played with his sisters but would much rather be playing with his Daddy.

Nancy: "He is always tugging at his father's trousers to get pushed around the yard in his go-kart. Give him a hammer and a screwdriver and he'll play by himself for hours."

Nancy produced a tender smile as she told the reporters how the children loved their father so much that Grant Snr. had to lock himself away if he wanted to read the paper.

"My husband bathed the kiddies and dried them. He always tickles Grant and makes him giggle when he is drying him. When this happens Arnna always gets jealous and wants to be tickled too. Jane wants to be tickled but she stands back and won't say anything when she sees the other two laughing."

The lightness in the conversation suddenly changed as Nancy stared into space thinking of Jane. "She is very particular about her body. This is why I can't understand these reports about a man being seen putting her shorts on over her bathers at the beach."

The Children "surely dead"

As the flow of fresh information about the case started to dry up, the media looked for new angles to the mystery. Academics were invited to make sense of the abduction.

Dr John McGeorge, Australia's leading criminal psychiatrist, told the press that the three missing Beaumont children were "surely dead".

McGeorge speculated that the children's killer had probably been inspired by the widely publicised "killings on the moors" in England (January 1966) and that one of the kiddies could have signed the death warrants of all three by using words like, "I'll tell on you!"

Dr McGeorge had a remarkable reputation for accurately predicting the outcome of Australian crimes.

Within three days of the kidnapping of Sydney schoolboy Graeme Thorne in 1960, Dr McGeorge predicted the boy would be murdered and described in uncanny detail what type of character the kidnapper killer would be.

Dr McGeorge concluded that whoever took Jane, Arnna, and Grant Beaumont away from the beach did so because:
- He had a grievance against the family or
- He wished to hold them for ransom or
- He was a psychopath or borderline mental case with a perverted twist.

The Beaumont family were neither rich or had any known

enemies and so the only conclusion that could be drawn from McGeorge's analysis was that a psychopath had been involved.

Dr McGeorge put forward a possible profile of the abductor. He believed the perpetrator was a "reserved, retiring character who lives either with aging parents or in a boarding house. He could be married but this is not likely. He has few if any friends and keeps much to himself. His intelligence would be limited and he would tend to act on impulse. He could be a labouring type or a not very skilled tradesman or clerk. He may have been before the Courts for some minor offences and got off lightly."

McGeorge's profile of the abductor could have been of some help if the police had a number 'persons of interest' to work with. However, after three weeks of the most intensive police investigation in the history of the South Australia, there was not one suspect. Not one piece of evidence of what became of the children had been uncovered.

The Truth

Jack 'Ace' Ayling, a respected reporter for the much maligned Melbourne newspaper, *The Truth*, was sent to Adelaide to delve into the Beaumont mystery.

When he and his photographer knocked on the door of the Beaumonts residence the couple were not at home but were greeted by Grant's mother Florence. She told them that Grant and Nancy had gone to the country.

Ayling was not called 'Ace' for nothing and soon found out that the Beaumonts had travelled to the mid north of the State for Grant's work.

3 The Man With the Crazy Walk

Ayling drove to a remote town and walked into the nearest pub, always a reliable source of information. Luck was on his side. The publican told him the Beaumont parents were staying in a nearby caravan park.

The Beaumonts were understandably hesitant and reluctant to talk at first but Ayling asked if he could buy them a drink and have a quick chat.

Ayling: "We had a couple of drinks and, during the course of the conversation, they finally confided: 'We believe the kids are still alive'."

Grant: "Look there's no reason to believe they're dead. We believe they're still around somewhere."

Nancy: "Why should they be dead? Why would anyone want to kill three kids? Why wouldn't they just want to snatch them or something and have a ready-made family?"

"Somebody could have taken the children to a woman who was desperate for children."

Nancy succinctly observed that there were in fact four people missing, not three. She said the man on the beach seen playing with the children had never come forward. In effect, he too was missing.

Grant then chimed in: "If he was only innocently playing with the children, why hasn't he come forward?"

The excited reporter phoned his editor with his story. In the next day's edition, *Truth* published a bold front page headline "Vanished three Beaumont Children 'Are Alive'."

The article also revealed that the Adelaide Homicide Squad had been taken off the investigation and it had been handed back to the local Glenelg CIB.

The Truth began an extensive publicity campaign to flush out clues and within a few days of the article an apparent breakthrough emerged.

Ray Gordon, a 50-year-old truck driver, claimed he saw two girls and a boy in the back of an old Ford utility on the highway between Adelaide and Melbourne just a few days after the Beaumont children disappeared. He said the driver of the utility fitted the description of the mystery man.

More witnesses emerged with similar sightings of the mysterious green utility with S.A. number plates and three children inside. The description of the driver tallied with the police identikit, except that his hair was no longer blonde but a light brown.

All of the sightings were made in the first three weeks of the case, but mysteriously none of the witnesses had come forward at the time.

The numerous sightings spanned a route from Adelaide to Albury. According to Ayling, "The time of the sightings were consistent with an abductor taking a slow trip south-east from Adelaide to Melbourne via Albury".

4
False Hope

Information regarding the Beaumont case continued to flow through to police, however their limited resources were being pushed and pulled in a number of unnecessary directions.

In February 1966, *The News* sensationally reported that they had received a phone call from a man who claimed he was holding the missing Beaumont children for ransom. The man with a foreign accent rang the newspaper and spoke to a telephonist and demanded a reward for surrendering the children.

"I want reward money for them. It will have to be a good reward."

The telephonist tried to connect him to the newspaper's editorial department, but the caller hung up before being transferred.

The next day Grant Beaumont's younger brother, Max, requested and was granted permission to sit in the editorial office of *The News* awaiting another call from the mysterious caller. Max, an interstate tourist bus driver, was desperate to help his family. He heard the shocking news of his brother's children on the radio while driving a bus-load of tourists in Tasmania.

Max Beaumont pleaded for the caller to contact him. "I have a special message from Grant and Nancy Beaumont. If the caller is genuine I'll come to any agreement he wants to get the children back." He went on to say he would meet any reward the caller demanded. "I don't know where it will come from but I'll raise it somehow."

Throughout his 12-hour stint Max received a number of calls with information but not the call he had wanted.

"There was not one new hoax call throughout the entire day."

"I am at a loss over what to do now. All I can do is wait."

A self proclaimed mystic was one of the few that talked to Max Beaumont and was fairly typical of the peculiar nature of calls the police and media were receiving.

"I am not the caller that rang yesterday but I have something to help you. I have been dabbling around with a glass on a table. It revealed that the children will be found with a German family in the Adelaide suburb of Newton."

Police not only had to sift through the information provided from crackpots they also had to follow up on reports from attention seekers.

Erwin Erhardt Grosser, 33, a labourer of Daveyston, was one of those.

Shortly after the children's disappearance, Grosser telephoned Freeling Police and claimed a man driving a Holden car with two girls and a boy as passengers had visited his home. He told police the children fitted the description of the Beaumonts and the man driving resembled the person being sought by police. He alleged the man produced a pistol from his pocket and forced him to fill the car radiator with water, before speeding off towards Nuriootpa.

Grosser later confessed to lying to police and claimed his sordid behaviour was due to being intoxicated at the time. Grosser said he had taken a keen interest in the case of the missing children and wanted police to test his theory the children had been taken out of the State via Renmark, a town on the banks of the Murray River.

Soon after Grosser's court hearing, a charge was laid against Raymond Lawrence Dunn, 42, of Tea Tree Gully, for having made a false report to the Whyalla CIB.

Police arrested Dunn on fraud charges and when he was brought into custody, police noticed that he bore a slight resemblance to the 'surfie' looking man wanted in connection with the missing Beaumont children.

Police questioned Dunn but he was deemed too inebriated to talk coherently. Next day, under questioning, he told the police he knew the whereabouts of the children and declared they were alive and well. He said a man and woman were holding the children captive in a house on the Esplanade at Glenelg. The Homicide Squad raided a number of homes in the area, before Dunn finally admitted he had lied. The woman involved was in fact his estranged wife who had run off with another man.

Grim Hunt
February 24, 1966

The general public in South Australia were doing what they were instructed to do — be alert and report anything unusual in their surrounds. Every piece of information about the children's disappearance was treated with urgency by police.

Detective A E Palmer (Head of SA Police Homicide Squad) and five detectives rushed to the beach at Hallett Cove to examine what was described as a "shallow grave" but it again proved to be a false alarm. When police began digging they only found dead branches.

That same afternoon Police attended the Marion Council rubbish tip after receiving a tip off that claimed a bag similar to the one Jane Beaumont carried and several pairs of children's bathers had been found. Fort Largs police cadets were once again called in to help with the search. The cadets, wearing overalls, long rubber boots, gloves, goggles and respirators to combat the whirling dust spent a day in filth but nothing was found in regards to the Beaumonts disappearance.

"Known to the family..."

As fresh developments slowed down to a trickle the media gradually began to stretch further afield for a 'story' regarding the children's disappearance. Newspapers and particularly television stations turned to 'experts' to fill the void.

On one such 'television special' Detective-Sergeant Palmer put forward a theory that a person "Known to the family fairly well in times gone by" may have abducted the three missing Beaumont children.

This was an important shift in focus as up until to this point the consensus was that a complete stranger had abducted the children; somehow enticing them into a vehicle after gaining their trust. S.A. Police were obviously widening the scope of their investigation scenarios.

During the television special a panel of police and experts discussed the various theories that were deemed plausible.

Palmer theorised, "It was quite possible that the man whom others had reported having seen with the children at the beach had made an arrangement to pick them up later, possibly in Jetty Road, Glenelg."

Det. Gollan said there were very few cases in S.A. where more than one child was taken by a pervert, but did not discount the theory that a sex offender planned such a crime. "Such a person would generally be of good education and appearance and a type whom children would trust. Many sex cases that involved children were premeditated."

Dr Salter: "It does suggest an elaborate plan. If it wasn't planned you would not expect him to take three children."

Palmer then put to Dr Salter a theory from left field. Palmer wanted to know "Whether a man, infatuated by a woman, would get to know her children and, to satisfy his desires, take the children away … and even look after them very well."

Dr Salter responded diplomatically to Palmer's curious scenario — "I think this is possible. A pervert usually has his own particular pattern."

Palmer obviously wanted a stronger confirmation. "Could

this be brought about by infatuation with a particular woman?"

Salter: "This is not a usual explanation but usually each pervert has his type of pattern set somewhere in his life and this tends to become fixed."

During February Grant Beaumont also revealed to the press another angle to the mystery. He said it was possible someone who knew of his business trips could have met the children and enticed them into a car. "He could have said: 'Why don't we all go and meet your daddy and give him a big surprise?'"

"The kids would have been tickled pink with a suggestion like that and anyone having managed to win their trust might have been able to get them away willingly."

Suspect Sketch for UK
April 19

Adelaide's daily tabloid newspaper, *The News*, reported that they had sent a full-length sketch of the police suspect in the Beaumont case to Scotland Yard. Scotland Yard believed a sketch drawn by an English art student wanted for the "Babes in the Ditch" murder was similar to the 'surfie' seen at Glenelg Beach.

On 12 January 1966, the bodies of Margaret Reynolds, age 6, and Diana Joy Tift, age 5, were found together in a ditch at Mansty Gully on Cannock Chase in Staffordshire. Reynolds went missing on her way to school in Aston, Birmingham, on 8 September 1965 and Tift went missing on a short walk to her grandmother's house in Bloxwich on 30 December that year. The girls had been strangled and sexually assaulted.

This was a tenuous link at best. There were less than four weeks between the last English murder and the Beaumonts disappearance. *The News* quoted a Migration Department officer in Adelaide who claimed that 645 assisted migrants had arrived in South Australia by air during January. The highly speculative connection dissipated within days.

"I know they're alive..."

Easter Sunday at the Beaumont family home had always begun with a traditional early morning 'Easter-egg hunt'. The night before, Nancy and Grant would plant chocolate eggs around the backyard for their delighted children to discover. As Easter approached in 1966 the Beaumonts had already planned a caravan trip to a West Coast (Eyre Peninsula) destination. The thought of staying at home without their children was incomprehensible. The couple departed Adelaide after spending a traumatic day with police at John Martin's department store. Nancy and Grant were asked to supervise the dressing of three childlike mannequins that were to be put on display at the Sydney Easter Show. The couple were visibly distressed as they were photographed with the lifeless looking mannequins.

After a 600 km drive from their West Coast getaway the Beaumonts arrived back at their Harding Street home late at night. As Grant parked the car, the headlights highlighted three bicycles hanging from the garage ceiling. They both stared at the girls two wheelers and little Grant's trike.

Everywhere Grant and Nancy looked there were signs of their lost children. Newspaper reporter, Ken Anderson who became close friends wrote a moving story just after they returned from their Easter trip.

Anderson, Nancy and Grant sat outside enjoying the morning autumn sunshine, sipping on their tea in their well kept suburban backyard. Grant pointed to the dormant children's swing. "Everything is there waiting for them". "We have not sold anything of theirs — the clothes, schoolbooks, toys … we have them all waiting for them to come back."

Grant was adamant in his belief that his three children were still alive. "Somebody has them somewhere. But we just don't know what kind of torture they could be going through."

Nancy: "They can't have just vanished off the face of the earth, nobody can do that. We go over and over it between ourselves and the logical thing seems to be that somebody has them — it could be a friend, or somebody we have never met."

"If they had got into a stranger's car it would only have been because the two younger children had talked Jane into it."

"I can see (Jane) her coming in here now and saying, 'Mummy, Arnna and Grant talked me into getting into the car, they made me do it.'"

"She would never get into a car on her own — but which car? Where did they go?"

Grant gazed at the brilliant blue sky. "In the mornings like this Janey would come creeping into the bedroom and say, 'Daddy, don't wake anybody else, you and I will go for a walk along the beach'."

Grant Beaumont's head bowed. "The children were my whole life. That's what a man marries for and builds a home and wants a future — for his children."

"Crossed line"
September 1966

Just when the case was turning cold a bizarre incident which involved a 'crossed' telephone line put the beautiful faces of the Beaumont children back on the front pages of Australian newspapers.

When a country Victorian policeman telephoned Russell Street Police Headquarters he heard another voice come on the line, "We're bringing the Beaumont kids back from Hobart". "We are tired and think it's time to give up."

Senior Constable Ron Grose, of Kaniva, situated 320 kilometres west of Melbourne near the South Australian border, immediately got in touch with the homicide squad who in turn, contacted S.A. detectives.

Grant Beaumont only heard of the incident when he read a brief article in *The News*. He immediately drove the 380 kilometres from Adelaide to Kaniva with television news reporter Brian Taylor, so he could talk to Senior Constable Grose, face to face.

Grant: "I wanted to get the information from Constable Grose first-hand. I wanted to get the truth from his eyes. Constable Grose gave me a real boost. I thought he was nearly in tears himself."

"He is certain the call is authentic. We know it must be true."

During their conversation Constable Grose revealed to Grant a curious fact; "Exclusive Brethren were very active in the remote areas surrounding Kaniva".

In Grant's mind this piece of information was vitally important as early in his children's disappearance there was a rumour from Tasmania that a religious sect known as 'The Exclusive Brethren' were holding the children captive. At the same time Tasmanian detectives had also made an all-out search for a man answering the description of the suspected blonde abductor who it was alleged was overheard talking about Adelaide to a young boy. However police were unable to track him down.

Grant: "It fits in perfectly."

Jack Ayling of *The Truth* newspaper contacted Detective Sgt Swaine, the chief of the Adelaide CIB to get his take on the 'crossed line' incident.

Swaine: "I'm certain that the crossed telephone conversation which policeman Ron Grose heard is genuine. It could be the first reasonable clue in the whole investigation."

Grant and Nancy Beaumont were naturally buoyed by the news of this breakthrough.

Grant: "We tried to figure out how these people could return the children to us without being caught. They would want to put a lot of miles between themselves and us before we got the children. Whenever they brought the children into public they would be seen, and police could get their descriptions. I think this is all that is delaying an end to this ghastly business — a shocking nerve-wracking nine months of our lives."

"I pray to God that it is ending."

Nancy: "More than ever now we are convinced someone is holding our children, and we appeal for them to be brought home. This is the first time we have had a solid, worthwhile clue since Jane, Arnna, and Grant were lost almost nine months ago.

Someone has got my children. I know it."

"I pray these people will be kind — kind to the children, and kind to us and return them."

"Please … please bring an end to all this suffering".

The new found optimism was soon deflated when the chief of the Victorian Homicide Squad, Det. Inspector Holland issued a statement declaring the police had investigated the incident "most thoroughly" and were convinced it could only have been a hoax.

"The hoaxer suggested that the call was made to or from Hobart, and the PMG assures us that there is no chance of a telephone call from Kaniva to Melbourne being crossed with a call from Melbourne to Hobart."

"We are not taking the matter seriously — except that we think it is a pretty despicable act to exploit such a tragedy for amusement." Holland explained that possibly somebody had accidentally got a crossed line, realised they were speaking to the police then "threw in the Beaumonts."

Two days later, the 'crossed line' telephone call had been traced. South Australian detectives revealed that they had interviewed two women involved with the telephone conversations and were satisfied the call had no bearing on the case; no charges were laid against them.

The revelation shattered Grant and Nancy's slim hope of a miracle.

5
1966: The Year of Lost Children

Apart from the tragic disappearance of the Beaumont children, 1966 was bizarrely filled with a number of instances of missing children in and around Adelaide. Some were runaways but other times the incidents were more sinister.

Six weeks after the Beaumont disappearance, two children were abducted by a man who "came to dinner." The father of the children had invited friends over for dinner and drinks; Douglas Ballis a 'friend of a friend' arrived as well and joined the party that turned into a boozy affair.

At about 8.30 p.m., a drunken Ballis told the host's nine-year-old daughter and her eight-year-old brother to go to his car and wait for him. Ballis then sped through the city streets to his rental unit, where he picked up his suitcases and blankets. He then drove to his employer's home and collected money that was owed to him. He told his boss the two children were his and that he was taking them to Western Australia because his wife had died.

Ballis headed north but made a detour to a side road near Virginia where he attempted to sexually assault the girl on the front seat of the car.

The girl screamed and cried hysterically causing Ballis to change his plans. The children were freed near the Port Wakefield Road where they were picked up by a passing truck driver.

Another incident in Adelaide involved a 3-year-old boy who had walked to a local deli with an eight-year-old neighbour at around 4.15 p.m. Outside the shop a man sitting in a car asked the boys to pick up a bottle lying on the footpath and give it to him. The older boy ignored the man and went into the shop but when he came out his younger friend had gone.

The 3-year-old was found later that night crying and wandering in a lonely stretch of sand hills at Semaphore six kilometres away along Military Road.

Glenelg had another 'Beaumont scare' when dozens of police patrols were swung into action to search for three small boys. The brothers had left home in the morning but failed to return home by nightfall.

What appeared to look eerily similar to the Beaumont abduction turned out to be a case of runaway children. The dramatic, widespread search went on through the night until the boys were found wandering in the Lockleys area about four miles from their home.

In October 1966 South Australia was once again confronted with a possible Beaumont-like abduction when two children were reported missing in the small coastal town of Port Elliot, 85 kilometres south of Adelaide. For two days an extensive search was conducted through the bushland. The search ended when the two children appeared from their 'hiding place'. They were found at midnight in a small farmhouse about a mile from their home.

Susan Wallach 13, and her brother, Richard, 10, had run away from their parents' pig farm at Crows Nest. Richard explained their reason for leaving home: "We have a lot of work to do around the farm, so we decided we would like to get away from it for a few days."

Susan: "Actually, we had decided to come home today when the food ran out."

Two days after the Port Elliot runaways were returned to their parents, another dramatic child disappearance challenged police.

The parents of eight-year-old Wendy Pfeiffer, reported her missing when she disappeared from the family farm at Mylor in the Adelaide Hills. The worried parents phoned police after the girl failed to return from taking the family dog for a walk. The dog returned to their home by itself.

For two days police manned a massive search in the bush without finding a trace of Wendy.

A breakthrough came when a sandal was found on a lonely bush track off Mount Bold Reservoir Road, several kilometres from her home.

The discovery of the sandal came after homicide detectives under the watchful eye of Det. Sgt. Stan Swaine had taken a 'person of interest' to the entrance of the track. The man, aged 22, had directed police to the possible whereabouts of the lost girl.

5 1966: The Year of Lost Children

Police then took the unusual step of charging him with murder without having found the girl's body. He had earlier admitted to his parish priest that he had abducted and stabbed the girl and left her to die.

Police were baffled at where the girl could be, even the police dogs could not find her, and called into action two Aboriginal trackers, Jimmy James and Daniel Moodoo. After 20 kilometres of tracking through thick bush the trackers found the girl stabbed to within a centimetre of her life.

She later described how the abductor had approached her as she walked her dog along the side of the road. He had asked her if she knew a good place for fishing and she told him "Yes Silver Lake". The man then pulled her into the car and onto the front seat and sped off. A short distance down the road he ordered her to keep quiet then stopped the car. The man produced a small knife and stabbed her in the chest three times. He had then driven off at speed and had turned into a side road where the shocked girl passed out.

She regained consciousness some time later to find herself lying alone in a thicket. One of her sandals was missing and her pants had been removed. She used her pants to place across her wounded chest and then walked into the thick scrub. She quickly became disorientated and headed in the opposite direction of her home.

Wendy described how during her ordeal she had watched lizards, snakes, and rabbits and drank from a creek to quench her thirst. Police estimated the brave little girl had walked 13 km through rugged bushland, when finally she could walk no further. Exhausted and in shock she managed to build a wind break then collapsed.

The abductor who pleaded not guilty, to the attempted murder due to insanity was found guilty by a jury and received a 12 year prison sentence.

The Pfeiffer parents were ecstatic to have their daughter back safe and well and received many phone calls and letters from people across South Australia relieved that the life of their child had been saved, however the most important communication came via a telegram — from Grant and Nancy Beaumont.

"We are very relieved and happy for you all — Mr and Mrs Beaumont."

Mr Pfeifer: "In this telegram they have expressed their heartiest congratulations. But their sorrow remains — a sorrow they have had for nine months."

6
Paranormal Detectives

Because of the peculiar nature of the disappearance of the Beaumont children it was inevitable that clairvoyants, visionaries, and unhinged theorists would come forward with unconventional theories on how the children had vanished.

These 'mystics' not only pestered the police and the press, they also relentlessly harassed Grant and Nancy Beaumont.

In February 1966 a self proclaimed 'spiritualist' Helmut Mueller; a resident of Nuriootpa, a small town in the Barossa Valley came forward with a theory. He claimed he had a 'vision' that the Beaumont children were buried at the bottom of cliffs in the seaside suburb of Marino, 8 km. south of Glenelg. The German migrant, who arrived in South Australian 10 years earlier, sparked a dramatic police search.

Mueller, an orchard farmer, told a reporter, "The spirits told me the Beaumont children were in a grave at Marino. I feel it through the ends of my fingers. They get itchy and nervous, and they told me where to find the grave yesterday."

He had reported his vision to the Elizabeth CIB, but after unsurprisingly not hearing from police, Mueller went to Marino to investigate for himself. He took his 'divining stick' with him.

"I walked along the beach with my stick … it pulled and tugged me towards the base of the cliff near the gully. The forces of the spirits became so strong they tugged at the stick and finally broke it."

"I knew this was the spot. It looked like a grave."

Mueller immediately drove to the nearest police station to report his find. Within an hour six police officers had rushed to the scene. The so called 'grave' turned out to be nothing more than a mound of earth.

The Beaumonts were so desperate for a breakthrough they were open minded to most people who claimed to offer a glimpse of hope about their children's whereabouts.

One morning Nancy opened the front door and was greeted by a woman standing on the porch with a pendulum hanging from her outstretched hand. Inside, the woman placed a map of Adelaide on the kitchen table and allowed the pendulum to dangle above it. After an hour or so Nancy's patience wore thin and politely sent her on her way.

There were occasions when the strangers who visited the Beaumont home were so upsetting the police had to be called.

Nancy, "I had one person who came to me in a religious mood with books and pamphlets about religion but I suppose you could say he tricked me. He called on me three or four times and from what he said I thought, 'Well he's a nice bloke?'"

However the 'nice bloke' was going behind Nancy's back, maliciously questioning her neighbours about her and her husband.

Nancy: "My neighbours rang the police and they [police] told him if he came on to my land again he would end up in gaol. And they asked him just exactly where HE was on January 26. He wrote great foolscap letters to the Police Commissioner. He turned out to be very nasty."

Not all of the people who contacted the Beaumonts during the months after their children disappeared were unhinged. Grant and Nancy received many heart warming letters from concerned people Australia wide and internationally offering their prayers and support; many of whom had been through tragedies of their own.

Nancy: "They put in their letters the things that had helped them to keep going in their own way — something to hold on to."

Nancy treasured a letter she received from the Somerton Park Brownies. "Jane belonged to this pack and I had a lovely letter from their lady leader. All the Brownies were out searching, those first couple of days. They made a little team effort which was very, very nice."

"People sent money in their letters … 20 cents, 50 cents, dollar notes."

"I know a lot of people meant well. They were very kind. But some people … I won't say they were sick … but when a person knocks on your door you just can't sum him up in a minute and decide. 'You're sick' or 'You mean well' or 'You don't'. You just listen."

"And I could see that with quite a few people, it was preying on their minds, and they meant well with their theories. But some of them were absolutely shocking. I stood there and listened."

"I don't like to be rude because you just never know who is talking to you."

Nancy admitted there were times when she became suspicious of the people who claimed to be helping her. "I was looking at them and wondering; I wonder if you've got anything to do with it?"

"For instance, that dreadful one about Sacred Heart College."

A male visitor to the Beaumont home had a far-fetched theory that the Brothers at the college had abducted her children, and that they were being held captive in an underground room. "He kept on in this vein, and when he had said his piece, he asked me. 'By the way, what religion are you?'"

"I said, 'I am a Catholic.'"

"He said 'I am terribly sorry' and shot off."

The Man with X-Ray Eyes

Australians first became familiar with the supposed clairvoyant powers of Gerald Croiset via Adelaide's local newspapers; *The News* and *The Advertiser*.

The 'Beaumont Mystery' was proving to be the biggest 'story' in decades; the media battle for an edge over its rivals was fierce. Both newspapers had their very own 'exclusive' Croiset informer.

The Advertiser's contact was in fact an employee who worked in the basement of the Advertiser building as a printer. Mr

Van Schie, a Dutch immigrant wrote to Croiset explaining the mystery to the renowned mystic. Croiset wrote back to Schie describing how he could 'see' the lost children and asked for more information to be sent to him.

Not to be outdone, *The News* uncovered a Dutch immigrant who had also corresponded with Croiset; Mr Karel Loof, of Brighton. The first vision of the seer was detailed in a letter he wrote to Loof.

Croiset's verdict was clear cut. "A tragic accident. No foul play".

"The children were playing innocently when there was some sort of collapse, a cave-in."

"They were fighting against sand or water and could not get out. Their bodies are lying near the surface on a stretch of open land not far from the beach."

Gerald Croiset was born on March 10, 1909, in the Dutch village of Laren. His parents were Jewish, his father an actor, and his mother a theatre dresser. For some unexplained reason, Croiset was handed over to foster parents as a toddler.

As a child Croiset often had visions. At 15 while working as a farmhand he 'saw' his father collapse in the centre of Amsterdam. When he arrived, two hours later, he was informed his father had died of a heart attack.

In an interview with the *Australian Women's Weekly*, Croiset revealed: "My forces are holy to me. Through them I try to provide the material by which science may be able to detect a new line in the psyche of human beings."

Croiset rapidly became the darling of the Australian press, who were only too eager to publish outlandish claims of his powers. In one interview he revealed that at least 350 children had been found as a result of his work! Incredibly, the local media did not scrutinise these implausible statements; they were simply accepted as fact.

"I am no wonder man, no magician. I have no supernatural forces. The only thing where I may be different is in the ability to tune in to others at the proper frequency and so get working contact with them."

As the publicity for Croiset's involvement in the Beaumont case ramped up, Croiset's 'visions' kept coming, and the Australian media lapped it up. He 'saw' the children's bodies lying in a cave among the rocks near the beach. "I see an overhanging rock plateau under which there are stones of a nice colour and behind which is a cave or hollow."

"Not far behind is some scrub and on the right-hand side a white house built in the form of a cube … "I see a dead animal between the stones, a bird or a dog…"

"In my opinion, the children crept to a hollow, closed off on one side… I see a hollow about half a mile from the spot where they have been seen last … In the distance, I see six separate houses, shells, or coral reef."

As cryptic as the clues may have sounded to most people, Croiset's Adelaide based supporters believed he had pin-pointed the area known as Minda Home.

Established in 1898, 'Minda', an Aboriginal word meaning place of shelter and protection, was the first facility in South Australia which provided residential support and education for people with intellectual disability. Located at Brighton, 3 km.

from the Beaumont's home, the site is approximately 28.5 hectares with 500m of coastal frontage.

The publication of Croiset's visions brought forward many theories on where the exact area could be however there was one particular hypothesis that sounded mildly plausible.

A Brighton undertaker, Doug Trevelion, came forward and claimed there was a 112-year-old family crypt buried in sand near the Minda Home that had an uncanny resemblance to the description of a likely burial place for the Beaumont children given by Croiset.

The crypt was built for members of the Featherstone family who owned property in the area during the 19th century. Eight bodies had to be removed from the crypt in 1954, when the roof collapsed.

According to records, the concrete tomb was approximately 8 ft. deep, 14 ft. long and 10 ft. wide. Entry could be gained by climbing through the partly demolished roof.

After news of the crypt was circulated by the media a number of people came forward with further information. One resident said that he had seen children climbing into the crypt as recent as December 1965.

Dozens of people were certain they knew where to locate the crypt but even with the help of bulldozers the mysterious crypt was never found. It had simply disappeared into the shifting sands.

The talk around Adelaide that a world renowned clairvoyant was taking an interest in the children's disappearance brought together people who were taking an active part in the search for the Beaumonts. The citizens of Adelaide especially in the suburbs near the children's disappearance had bandied together as one to help solve the case.

The spokesperson for the group was Dr Hendrickson. He recovered three items mentioned in a Croiset vision, and sent photographs to Holland indicating where the items had been found.

The items — a battered straw hat, the remains of a dead bird and a piece of black material — were found a short distance apart at the edge of the oval in the grounds of Minda Home.

On September 9, 1966 newspapers headlines across Australia proclaimed Croiset had confirmed he would be coming to Adelaide to help with the Beaumont children mystery.

Asked in Utrecht, Holland, if he felt confident of finding the bodies of the missing children, Croiset said: "I am never 100 per cent sure; I can only do my best."

The cost of bringing Croiset to Adelaide was going to be shared between two Adelaide businessmen.

Barry Blackwell, a young managing director of Midway Motors of Brighton, agreed to pay half of Croiset's airfare. He had already contributed to the cost of hiring a helicopter so that photographs of the Glenelg beach-front could be taken and sent to Croiset. He also generously donated $2,000 towards a reward for information about the abduction. Blackwell came forward after the Melbourne newspaper; *The Truth* increased its reward to $5000.

Blackwell was upset at the news that Grant Beaumont had planned to sell his home to contribute to the reward fund. The

Beaumonts had purchased their home through the War Service Loan scheme.

Grant Beaumont: "If we found them we would willingly give it up and start with them again somewhere else. After giving away the $4,000 we would be pretty broke, but at least we would have the children."

Blackwell was angry at the State Government's initial meagre reward. "Mr Beaumont should never have to give that [his home] away."

Blackwell's public commitment to a reward for information kept him busy with phone calls from the general public. So much so he kept a tape recorder on his office desk ready to record any conversation that had relevance to the Beaumont mystery.

Blackwell: "There is a chance that somebody will ring. I've got to be ready."

One of the phone calls he received unsettled him. "The voice was bitter, sneering, insulting." The caller hung up but rang back soon after.

"You reckon you got $2000?"

Blackwell: "Not on me, but I could soon have it."

There was an extended silence before the caller hung up.

Blackwell also organised an extensive search of storm drains by 'frogmen' wearing breathing apparatus. Searchers had tried to reach deep into the massive pipes earlier but were forced back by strong fumes.

The reason Blackwell had concentrated his efforts on the storm drains was that while he was talking to the Beaumont parents they mentioned that the children had recently enjoyed playing in the large painted drainpipes at Veale Gardens in the CBD parklands.

Also helping with the expenses was businessmen, Con Polites, a property tycoon who apparently knew Nancy Beaumont when she was single and working at an O'Connell Street business in North Adelaide.

Polites was a glowing example of a self made man. Born in the regional town of Port Pirie, he left school at 15 to open a corner deli; he then relocated to Adelaide where his entrepreneurial skills soon turned to property. Con was not shy about his wealth. His properties were like his cattle, branded for all to recognise. Every property he owned had a distinctive 'POLITES' sign in the Greek national colours of blue and white, bolted to the building. He rarely sold.

November 7, 1966

The News who claimed to have exclusive access to Croiset during his visit to Adelaide produced a bold headline banner quoting the psychic — "I WILL FIND THEM IN TWO DAYS".

"I have had a vision of where the children started from. I will walk there and a vision will come to me immediately. I am 90 per cent sure I will pinpoint the place where the bodies will be found."

Journalists, photographers and TV cameramen from all over Australia once again converged on Adelaide for Croiset's attempt to solve Australia's most baffling mystery.

When Grant Beaumont was asked whether he would like to greet the mystic at the airport, he bluntly replied. "What kind of parents would we be, greeting the man who believes our children are dead?"

"If he wants to meet us, that will be fine, but it will be in private. Mr Croiset has been coming on and off for six months, and the doubt about it all has been most upsetting to us. We would like to see him come and to get it over with, whatever he is going to do."

Croiset finally arrived in South Australia, and was greeted by close to two thousand people who lined the Adelaide Airport terminal viewing platform. The crowd included over 100 reporters and a large and enthusiastic contingent from the Dutch community who had settled in Adelaide.

The following morning (November 8, 1966) Con Polites chauffeured the mystic to the 'scene of the crime', the Glenelg beach foreshore.

Croiset was a tall man with the appearance of a 'mad professor'. He had thick, un-kept curly hair, a large protruding nose with fierce intense eyes. He roamed around the grassed area of Colley Reserve alone with a camera hanging from his neck. He wore a dark crumpled suit, and carried with him a sizeable tape recorder and note-pad.

Polites, Blackwell, Dr Hendrickson and the physic's interpreter, Mr Smeding, watched Croiset's every move from a distance as he wandered around the beautiful beach-side surrounds.

Croiset paid particular attention to the 'side show alley' area situated close by. He took a number of photographs of the merry-go-round, then walked 50 metres south and took photographs of the general beach scene and the buildings along Jetty Road. In a little over an hour, Croiset had taken 42 pictures of objects and scenes which he claimed were scenes from his visions back in Holland.

The psychic rested for 15 minutes on a white wooden bench, the same bench that the elderly witness had sat on when she had observed the children and the 'surfie' suspect.

A party of over 50 pressmen followed Croiset as he began walking south along the Esplanade past the old Pier Hotel. His route then took him along College Street to Moseley Street. He walked briskly until he arrived at the intersection of Robert Street. At this point he was half-way to the Beaumont home on a direct route.

When he arrived at the delicatessen on the corner of Moseley and Robert Streets, Croiset suddenly paused and signalled to his interpreter and other members of the party to keep their distance.

He then slumped against a brick wall, with his eyes closed and head bowed. After a few minutes he sat on the steps at the side of the shop and furiously began making notes, occasionally hanging his head between his legs apparently in deep contemplation. Croiset then rose quickly and started walking back towards the beach. He excitedly revealed a new vision to his interpreter. He had 'seen' a cube house with a yellow van out the front. What this 'vision' had to do with the children was not revealed.

He then signalled to Polites, who fetched his car. Polites picked up Croiset in his Rolls Royce and then sped through the side streets of Glenelg as he tried unsuccessfully to shake off the pack of media representatives who followed in pursuit.

Croiset eventually found what he was looking for; a 'cubic' house at the corner of Elgar and Brighton Roads. It had a yellow van in front of it.

During a lunch break at a local hotel, Croiset had yet another vision. He abruptly stopped eating and motioned for a piece of paper. Croiset then drew four sketches; a small schoolhouse, a road cutting, two posts lying on the ground with another post lying across them, and a fence with part of the foreshore. In the last sketch there was a cross marking the spot where Croiset believed the children would be found.

Polites was astounded with Croiset's powers and believed the mystic's knowledge of unknown terrain could not have been feigned. Polites was also impressed in how Croiset had come to Adelaide with no known ulterior motive.

Polites: "I asked him how much I could pay him. He said, through an interpreter, 'You have insulted me. I don't want any money. I've come out here to find the children'."

"Now how can you not like a man like that?"

The next day Croiset became highly energised in his movements when it was revealed to him that a vacant block of land he saw in another 'new vision' had been discovered by a *News* reporter.

The block, only a few hundred metres from the Minda Home, had an old pit in the centre covered with boxthorn and tree boughs.

Later in the day Croiset made another search of the Minda Home area and amazingly found the old disused pram that he saw in his vision in Holland. The clairvoyant found the pram wedged between the northern boundary fence of Minda Home and a back yard shed on neighbouring property.

While Croiset wandered the streets, the Beaumont parents were at their home quietly going about their business as normally as they could. Grant's weekly business trip with Nancy, was put on hold for the week. Grant: "I couldn't have done anything. We were too upset."

"I will point to exact spot"

On the night of November 10th, Croiset was resting in his hotel room, deflated at his lack of success, when he received a phone call from Polites.

Polites revealed that a woman had phoned his secretary and told her that she believed the children could be buried at a warehouse near her home.

The next morning a press conference was held where Croiset sensationally asserted the children were buried 9ft deep near the wall of a store room at Paringa Park, only 500 metres from the Beaumont's home.

Soon after the sensational claim was made, the Deputy Commissioner of Police, Mr Leane sent police officers to accompany Croiset to the warehouse, situated at the corner of Wilton Avenue and Brighton Road.

The warehouse was a dilapidated, empty building in January but had been rebuilt in the last two months.

The news of the 'Beaumont breakthrough' spread like wildfire. Crowds of people converged to the area in a frenzy of expectation. An urgent call for police back-up was made to help control the crowd as it grew larger by the minute. Cars were lined up for hundreds of metres along Brighton Road and Wilton Avenue. People began to spill onto the busy roads.

Croiset was visibly shocked when he arrived at the warehouse with Detectives O'Brien and Zeunert. The crowd was so large he was at first reluctant to leave Polites' car.

Police escorted Croiset into the building where he spent several hours inspecting the store. A brick kiln was on the site until a few months ago and employees at the factory said a number of holes had been filled in recently.

Croiset was emotive as he stood in the middle of the storeroom. He claimed he received his strongest 'feeling' situated in a circle near the inner wall of the building.

"This is why in my first vision in Holland I saw the sea, merry-go-round and a bunker."

"When I got to the merry-go-round at Glenelg and saw everything fitting in. I looked for this bunker, about which I had a very strong emotion."

"I found it. I had confused a toilet block with a bunker which looked similar in Holland. In this bunker I had seen the elder girl taking off some of her under clothes."

"I found the yellow truck and the advertising sign I had seen in my previous visions."

"I found the hardware shop, and there I had to make up my mind what to say about this."

"I had to consider that if somebody had poured concrete into the foundation hole where the children were, the builders would have a fear that they were responsible. You probably noticed I sat down by myself and had a real fight with myself."

"Was I going to disclose this and set this fear going?"

"I came away very dejected and decided to leave Adelaide and be called a bad seer."

"Then came a telephone call and I spoke to a woman and her husband at their home in Wilton Avenue, Somerton Park."

"I suddenly realised what they were telling me was true."

He said he believed the three children had gone to the building the night they disappeared looking for shelter. "They were looking for shelter near friends." He then controversially stated, "They were afraid to go home."

Nancy, Grant and Croiset

Grant and Nancy Beaumont met Croiset just before he left South Australia to embark on another 'search' in the United States.

Understandably the meeting between the parents and the physic was initially cool; however the Beaumonts soon became welcoming and warm. As a token of goodwill they graciously presented Croiset with a kangaroo leather writing case.

They sat in the sunshine on the patio in the Beaumonts back garden and talked to each other through an interpreter. Dozens of reporters, photographers and television cameramen watched on close by.

Grant was forthright with his first statement: "You have your feelings like everybody else and I have my beliefs, and I believe my children are alive."

Croiset: "I hope you are right."

Grant: "Until there is any evidence they are not alive, my wife and I will go on believing they are alive."

Croiset: "Until they have been found you go on believing they are still alive. I will do my utmost to help you."

Croiset: "I have children of my own and understand your suffering. We are all children of God and you have to trust Him."

"I try to be in the employ of God and I try to do the best if can."

Grant: "We appreciate you coming over here and we are very

grateful to everyone concerned."

The meeting was over within 15 minutes. Grant later told a reporter. "He has failed but he did his best."

Although the Beaumonts were always sceptical of Croiset's abilities they were certainly won over by his charm. They both agreed that "He's a thorough gentleman."

To dig or not to dig?

After the departure of Croiset the South Australian Government had a serious challenge to contend with.

Would they listen to a physic and dig up the newly built warehouse using taxpayer's funds? Would they concede to the overwhelming public opinion who were now calling for action and put to rest Croiset's claims? Or would they look at the physics claims and denounce them as implausible.

S.A. Police investigated the claims and interviewed people who knew and remembered the old warehouse as it was back in January, 1966. They then handed a report on their findings to the South Australian Premier, Frank Walsh.

In late November, Premier Walsh quashed any government involvement in an excavation. "Investigations have shown conclusively, without a shadow of doubt, that there is no possible chance the factory is the burial ground of the missing children."

"I believe an excavation at this site would prove fruitless."

The government's stand on the warehouse dig only galvanised the many people who demanded an excavation.

A Citizens Action Committee was formed. They conducted a poll on whether the warehouse floor should be excavated. The committee claimed it received 13,000 Yes votes.

Buoyed by the outstanding positive vote they called for public subscriptions to fund the costly venture.

Mr Dawson (the head of the committee) told reporters, "I know many people, particularly women, feel the Government has left the case up in the air. They feel the warehouse should be excavated."

"The bodies of the children would be found under the floor of Woolcocks Discount House ... They were afraid to go home. The children had sheltered near a fence, crawled into a hole for protection, and this had collapsed."

Dawson claimed Croiset had initially looked for rocks while he was in Adelaide but, "They turned out to be the pieces of concrete he had seen at the site."

By March 1, 1967 the funds for the excavation project were available. Workers used a water-cooled diamond cutting machine to demolish the cement floor of the Paringa Park warehouse. Within two hours, 60 ft of cement has been cut away.

The next day workmen excavated a 12 ft by 8 ft area reaching a depth of 10 ft in some parts; the goal of the dig was to reach a depth of 12 ft.

As in most excavation work there were unknown obstacles waiting to delay the process. The dig uncovered a conveyor belt used in a brick kiln, a disused staircase and a large hoper bin, one of two under the warehouse.

Workmen used crowbars, shovels and jack hammers until they finally reached the depth of 12 ft. over a 20 ft by 8 ft area.

The items found during the dig were; a piece of towelling shirt cuff, lolly papers, insulation tape, lunch wrappings, lemon peel, and newspapers dated 1965. All items were handed to police for testing by the Police Forensic Laboratory.

During the dig, a reporter noticed a familiar face standing next to a car watching intently at a distance; it was Grant Beaumont.

Grant: "I drove down to the area for a simple reason — I wanted to see what the people were doing and how many were there."

"I felt terrible … I only stayed there for about five minutes."

"What are my feelings about people who watch that sort of thing? Well they're like people who want to look at accident victims. What do you call them … Ghouls?"

Dawson released a statement on behalf of the Citizens Action Committee. "A useful purpose has been accomplished by carrying out the express wish of the public who of their own accord said that excavations should be carried out to remove for once and for all a nagging doubt concerning the whereabouts of the children."

The lack of success in the costly excavation did not deter Gerald Croiset who during a telephone call with a News Ltd. journalist stated "My vision has not changed." He implored the committee to get the workers to dig a further three-feet deeper; however the dig came to a predictable end without any further knowledge into the disappearance of Jane, Arnna and Grant.

Police secretly dig

Only a day after the Paringa warehouse excavation ended, a Melbourne newspaper reported that police had been digging in the Adelaide Hills for the missing children.

The information came from Sydney clairvoyant, Mr Marinus Dykshoorn who gave the police a location to dig and a description of a man he believed was involved.

S.A. Police Inspector Eaton admitted the digging took place a few weeks earlier but "Nothing came of them".

Dykshoorn had met with police after spending two days retracing the Beaumont children's steps around the suburbs of Glenelg and Somerton Park. He claimed he received "Clear impressions of pictures and people and places. I follow up these leads like a police dog looking for a scent".

His tool of trade was a divining rod — a piece of twisted wire. "This helps me to concentrate."

Dykshoorn claimed to have found an incredible 200 bodies for police and relatives while working as a "paragnost" in Europe.

He arrived in Australia in 1960 with his official passport stamped "clairvoyant" as his occupation.

7
The One Pound Note

January 26, 1967

On the first anniversary of their children's disappearance, Grant and Nancy left their home to escape the distressing media coverage about to unfold. They drove north pulling their trusty caravan all the way to Jamestown, a pretty town 200 kilometres north of Adelaide.

Tom Prior, the veteran *Sun* reporter somehow tracked them down while they were trying to unwind at the caravan park. True to their giving nature, Grant and Nancy invited Prior to stay for dinner.

During the conversations, Grant Beaumont described the hurt they both felt at Christmas; the first without their children.

"Every day is bad enough, but I just couldn't stand Christmas. Everywhere you looked there were people taking presents home to their kids."

Grant and Nancy decided to flee the silence and trauma of

their home and headed for Sydney, but only got as far as Mildura; a regional city in north-western Victoria. They camped at the local caravan park.

Christmas in 1966 was terribly hot and no matter where they stayed the memories of their loss haunted them.

Grant: "We just couldn't stay in the caravan looking at each other. Outside we'd see the other mothers and fathers playing with their kids and the kids trying out their Christmas presents. We got in the car and we were home by Boxing Day. But there was nothing at home."

"These have been terrible days for us … you can imagine how empty our house was. Nobody in this world can understand what we are going through. You just can't understand. You can't…".

Nancy: "Jim and I are convinced the children are alive, I know I said I believed they had been murdered the week they disappeared, but I was sick then. The doctor had kept me asleep, but if the children had been murdered, their bodies would have been found. You couldn't hide three bodies, and who would murder three children?"

Grant: "It's with us all the time. Our children are alive. Nance and I would go mad if we didn't believe that."

"I know there are a lot of maniacs in the world, but, if you knew my kids, you'd known that even a maniac couldn't do them any harm." "A man or a woman, or probably a man and a woman together, persuaded them to get into a car and drove them away somewhere. They might have told them Nance and I were killed in an accident, and they've got them somewhere. It would have to be on a station or some isolated place like that."

Grant went on to describe how cruel some people had been

towards them. "People have said that Nance and I aren't married, that the children aren't Nance's, or mine, and that one of us has hidden them away from the other. One of us is supposed to be a member of the Plymouth Brethren who has kidnapped the children."

"My god, if they could only see what it is doing to Nance and me. It is no good without children, not when you have had them I just can't understand life without my kids. There is no point to it. You know, I couldn't even go into the yard outside without those kids following me and trying to start up a conversation."

Grant showed the reporter a package of 20 photographs he kept close to his heart, in a crumpled envelope in his coat pocket. The assortment of photos featured his children at the zoo, playing with their pet dog, Grant jnr. in his father's gardening boots, and all three of them helping their father dig a garden bed in the backyard. Every photo displayed happiness, contentment and joy.

Nancy's Dream

For twelve long and excruciating months the Beaumont parents had suffered indescribable stress waiting for news of their three children.

Amazingly, Nancy still had hope. "The longer this goes on, the more confident I feel that they are still alive. Do you know, I dreamed about them last night. I don't usually dream; in fact this is the first real dream I've had since the children went. But last night I dreamed I heard a knock on the back door. It was the children. They said, 'Hello, Mum'. The only thing I said was, 'Where have you been?'"

"They were standing there in the back lobby. I cried, and felt them all over."

Wenzel's Cake Shop

On the anniversary of the children's disappearance, Sgt. Blight, the officer in charge of the investigation finally revealed a significant breakthrough. It was divulged that the Beaumont children, who had left their Somerton Park home with 7/6 (75 cents) in silver coins in a white purse, bought their lunch at a Wenzel's Cake Shop with a one pound note.

How the children obtained the one pound note is an intriguing question.

An employee of the Wenzel's cake shop at 2 Moseley Street, Glenelg, was certain the three children were in the shop between 11.30 a.m. and 11.45 a.m. on January 26 — the day the children disappeared.

The cake shop fronts the bus stop on Moseley Street where the children were to catch a bus to their home.

Det. Blight said that when the children left home Nancy Beaumont had given them just enough coins to buy pasties for their lunch and for their bus fare.

The Beaumont parents also confirmed that the children regularly bought their lunch at Wenzel's shop.

Blight: "Grant is one of few children who won't eat pasties. Just as the eldest of the three children was to pay for their lunch the youngest, a boy, asked: 'Where is my pie?'"

Det. Blight said the children bought five pasties, one pie, six buns and two large bottles of soft drink at the cost of 11/-.

7 *The One Pound Note*

The shop employee, after seeing photographs of the Beaumonts in the newspapers on January 27, told fellow workers at the shop she had served the same children the day before.

The employee of the cake-shop was emphatic the three children were the missing Beaumonts.

Blight: "If they were the kiddies, it could be the key to the mystery."

This 'one pound note' mystery was certainly intriguing. However the children's order of five pasties, one pie, six buns and two large bottles of soft drink, does not sync with the children's requirements. So was it the Beaumont children or was it another set of three children with no significance to the abduction whatsoever?

The police became aware of this piece of information on January 27, 1966; why had they kept it under wraps for 12 months? Holding back this 'clue' from the public was one of the few known shortcomings by the detectives working on the case. If the information was given to the media at the time, while people's memories were fresh, there could have been a definitive answer to the identity of the children with the one pound note.

September 5, 1967

Mike Coward, a *News* journalist (later to become a world renowned cricket writer) reported that the head of the Homicide Squad, Det. Sgt. Stan Swaine had a fresh lead in the case.

Swaine: "We are re-checking one aspect of the case which was reported to us soon after the children disappeared."

An Adelaide psychiatrist who had been interviewed by police

revealed to Coward that a man who was admitted to the Glenside Hospital a few days after the children disappeared.

The man in question was described as a "schizophrenic with sex-deviate tendencies". The psychiatrist said the man had an obsession with the disappearance of the children, "Well before the general hue and cry had started."

According to the psychiatrist the man was also obsessed with digging up floors. The doctor claimed the man's family lived within a few hundred metres of the Beaumont home, and at the time of the children's disappearance the man lived alone in Durham Street, Glenelg; one street away from the Glenelg foreshore where the children were last seen.

According to the newspaper report, his description supposedly matched that of the '6ft. surfie' seen playing with the children.

The psychiatrist first reported his suspicions to police in January 1966 but police told him that they had received hundreds of reports similar to his. "There were also many patients at Glenside at the time who claimed to know something about the children, but this man had a genuine obsession about them … He seemed to know as much about them that it was felt the police should be told."

The doctor also claimed the man in question had been a voluntary patient at Glenside, "Which is most unusual for a schizophrenic".

One day later *The News* reported, "It is now understood the man does not resemble another man believed to have met the children at the beach. The man is about 21, single and walks with a stoop." Another potential lead that led to another dead-end.

8
"There is somebody in this world who knows something"

February 1968

After two years of unimaginable suffering, Grant and Nancy Beaumont decided to allow newspaper journalists (Ken Anderson, Doug Easom, and Brian Francis) back into their home so that the public interest in their missing children would not wane. This would be the last time Grant and Nancy would discuss their children in depth for nearly 25 years.

The News produced an outstanding insight into the courageous yet tormented lives of Grant and Nancy. The series of articles began with an emphatic Grant Beaumont pleading for someone to come forward with information.

"There is somebody in this world who knows something. A person or persons have the children. I believe the children are alive. It could be a very kind person who has them. He or she probably loved children and is looking after them. It could be a man or woman or both."

Grant speculated how the perpetrator may have told the children that he and Nancy were killed in an accident. "They could have said to the children: 'We have come to look after you — come with us'!"

The two parents discussed how they always wanted children, and were over the moon when their firstborn, Jane, arrived on September 10, 1956.

Nancy: "Jane was a very intelligent little girl; very bright."

"Arnna, well she just knew she had to go to school but she was a great little singer, always dressing up. Arnna lived more in a little fantasy world of her own. She wasn't a loner, though. She always got Grant and Jane in with her and would have them all dressing up."

"Grant was a very bright little boy ... He was more like Jane, very quick to pick up anything and I think he would have been very bright at school. He was a little gentleman too."

Grant Beaumont glowed with pride when he described how his little son often helped him maintain the family car. "He knew everything I told him about the car. When I changed the wheels he used to help me."

Nancy: "As for the three kiddies together — it was rather lovely. They were very kind to one another and they were always together. There was no bitterness."

Nancy recalled how excited the two girls were when baby Grant arrived home: "It was the best thing that had ever happened to the girls in their lives. They treated him like that all through — just like a doll. They nursed him and bathed him and things like that."

8 "There is somebody in this world who knows something"

When the couple were questioned about the children's future dreams, Nancy replied with pride in her voice: "Jane wanted to be a writer. An author of all things, it was odd at that age even to think of that, but she was very keen on writing and she was very good too."

Nancy: "She was also very keen on poetry — not so much adventures, but a little bit of fantasy, too. She would notice the flowers and trees and things like that and write about them. They were lovely little pieces and very, very descriptive. She had a lovely mind that way."

Nancy told the reporters how her children were infatuated with a make-believe horse.

"They used to ride on a 'saddle' on a branch of a tree in the back yard. Oh yes, he was down there all right. He was there in their minds. They had a bucket of water for him and plenty of grass for him to eat — dry, not green grass."

The 'fantasy horse' at one stage became a serious line of investigation into the children's disappearance. One of Jane's school friends revealed to police how Jane had often talked about the 'horse' and had said it was kept in a stable in the Somerton Park area because it had 'grown too big' for their home. Jane had told her friend that she and her brother and sister often visited the stable.

The stable in question was investigated but nothing came of this lead.

The subject of likes and dislikes of food was raised. Nancy shook her head and smiled.

"Grant was a shocking eater..."

Nancy revealed that the only way she could entice young Grant to eat, was by placing the little boy on a swing, "As he came forward each time I would pop the spoon in his mouth. He wouldn't care if he never ate."

Grant was also adverse to soap and water.

Grant: "He loved the beach but he didn't like having a wash. If you wanted to keep something from Grant, the safest place to hide it was under the soap." Grant's weathered face grimaced with a painful smile.

As far as the beach was concerned, Nancy Beaumont admitted she went along on such outings under sufferance, "I don't like the beach."

Grant Beaumont was the complete opposite. "Every day I was home and it was warm enough to be beach weather I would be down there with them. We used to get up at six in the morning and I would take them down — usually the Broadway, which is about half way between home and Glenelg itself."

"They were normal children. Sideshows were their idea of part of a day at the beach, but I used to try and keep them away from there. They would have their little paddling boards, but of course Grant didn't like going out so deep. He used to cry because I was out there with the girls a bit deeper. So I would have to go and lie on the shore, to please him, you see. I would keep an eye on the girls."

The interview took a more sombre turn when the parents were asked yet again for the descriptions of what the children were wearing that day. Nancy's head bowed as she spoke.

"Jane was wearing pink bathers, green shorts, and canvas tartan sandals. Grant had little green striped bathers and shorts and little red sandals."

"It was really hot the day before. That's why little Grant, for instance, didn't have a singlet or a shirt.

8 "There is somebody in this world who knows something"

"I thought they would be home in a few hours. I know what little ones are like. They wouldn't be bothered with underclothes."

"I thought, they'll just get off the bus. It's hot and they'll dry off and get back on."

"I know perhaps other people think it's rather odd to send kiddies to the beach not fully dressed. But down here you don't take any notice of that."

"They knew the beach very well. They had been before like this. They had been on their bikes before. The girls each had two wheelers and Grant a three wheeler. On their bikes, they would go to the Broadway. But the bus stops right in the heart of Glenelg, you see."

"Naturally, they were not going to walk back to the Broadway. They would swim close handy so that they could go to the shop, get a drink, and then back on the bus."

Nancy Beaumont was asked to retell the horror of January 26, 1966.

"I can't remember who was up first that day. Jane was the early riser. When I say she'd be first up. She wouldn't necessarily be first out of bed. She'd be first to wake, but she'd read, you see. But the other two were the ones! As soon as they woke up they would be up and into my room. Jane would read first and then come in."

"They all used to make their own beds and dress themselves. They were good little kiddies that way. I'm not wrapping up my own children, but they were capable kiddies even though they were little. I have always taught them to do things — dress themselves, make beds, little things like that."

"It wasn't that I didn't want to do it myself, it's just that I organised them into that routine."

Nancy told the reporters that soon after 8 o'clock the children had eaten their breakfast and were dressed for the beach. They were eager to get on their way. Nancy had chores to do and urged them to be patient. It was always her intention she would go to the beach with them.

The children's impatience got the better of her so she agreed they could go alone. After farewelling her children, "I came back inside and did a few jobs. Then about half-past 10 or somewhere about there I rode my bike over to see a girlfriend of mine. She lives just the other side of Diagonal Road."

"I left her place about five to 12 to meet the bus."

"They weren't on the bus, but I wasn't particularly worried. The bus might have left a minute early, or the kiddies might have been a minute late and there wasn't another one until 2 o'clock."

"So I went on home."

"A couple of friends of ours dropped in unexpectedly."

"It was just after two I started to worry. I had these visitors here, you see, and I was talking away. I commented at the time that I was a little worried that the kiddies hadn't arrived home on the two o'clock bus."

"My friends offered to go down and have a look, but I said, 'Well there's not much point in that because if they have decided to walk, which they have done before, we won't know which street there coming along — Moseley Street, Partridge Street or Brighton Road."

"And if they're on the bus we'll miss them, anyway."

"So I said, 'Its best we wait for the 3 o'clock bus'."

"So I just stayed there."

"The next thing, Grant came in."

Grant: "When I arrived, Nan was worried that the children weren't home."

Nancy: "He said to me. 'They'll be all right. They'll be home. You would have heard if anything was wrong by now.'"

Grant Beaumont remembered rushing to the beach. "There were so many people that I wouldn't have seen the kiddies if they were there. This was about half past three. Then I came back home again myself to see that I hadn't missed the children. But they still weren't home."

"That decided us. Nan came with me and we went and search again then we reported it to the police at Glenelg."

Nancy recalled the anxiety she experienced and the subsequent numbness once she was administered with drugs to help her sleep.

Nancy: "I'm a bit blank on things for about a fortnight after. The doctors were coming here for about a fortnight voluntarily, you know. "I was vague."

Grant: "You were out for a week. Over a week."

Nancy was asked about her initial thought and fears.

"Even at 5 o'clock I thought they were overstaying their day at the beach. And I thought they would even catch the 5 o'clock bus. And when it came nightfall — to be honest — I thought: 'There is only one reason the kiddies are not home — somebody is holding them aback stopping them from getting here.'"

"And then I thought they had fallen down a big hole or something — over the cliffs, perhaps, in the dark. That was what was going through my mind."

"Kidnapping never entered my mind. After all, they were three children together. If there was only one … perhaps that would have entered my mind."

"But, who would think in a million years that anyone would kidnap three?"

Grant: "I thought they had met some total stranger and he had befriended them and enticed them into a car. I ruled out drowning altogether."

The *News* reporters questioned the couple about the 'hate mail' they had received.

Grant: "There was a rumour that we weren't married and that the children weren't ours. I didn't bother listening to them."

Nancy: "That's right. Even if I was married, they said they weren't children of our marriage, and I had lived with people before. There wasn't an ounce of truth in any of it. Of course the police had checked on us."

"And then Grant was supposed to be the taxi-driver who faked a hold-up and shot a bullet into his own cab."

Grant: "They got me mixed up with somebody else, that's all."

"But people talk among themselves and elaborate. By the time it goes to three or four people it can get very nasty. Many of my friends have had arguments about some of the things they've heard."

"Even neighbours have told them things and now they're not on speaking terms."

Nancy: "People don't actually say these things to us personally. They haven't got the stomach to come and face you with this talk."

"The kiddies are missing and they forgot that. They forget to keep looking. They would rather dig the dirt. That's how I see it…"

Grant: "The Sunday drivers come past. You can always see them from the garden. They come past at five miles per hour, all looking in our direction, and you can almost hear them saying, 'This is where the Beaumont children lived'."

"They've even got children in the car."

"I call them the five-miles-an-hour convoys."

Not all the curiosity came from sightseeing motorists.

When Nancy first ventured outside her home many weeks after the children's disappearance she was well aware of people's unmasked stares.

"I tried to carry on normally. But it's very hurtful to be stared or pointed at."

"You just sort of feel that you must put your chin up a little higher and try."

"You have to go out and you have to mix with people, whatever they are thinking. I did not go out for some time, but I realised that if you stay inside too much you get too frightened to go out."

"You get frightened of people and once that gets hold of you, and then you get sick. So I had to go out and be among people. That was a big help to me; it was hard to do — to go out and try to be normal and have a lot of people around me."

"Even if I might have been bored stiff, at least they were there."

The Beaumont parents revealed that they had been given an amazing amount of support in their troubled times.

Nancy: "Everyone we knew around here — our neighbours and the postman, the baker, the milkman, and all the other tradesmen — was very upset."

"We don't talk about it when we meet because we can't come up with an answer."

"So we are only knocking ourselves around by going on and on about it. But they do feel. I know that because they have been so kind."

Grant: "And the police, they couldn't have done more than they did. They are all gentlemen. They are doing their job and doing it to the best of their ability."

"Anything I have wanted checked out or anybody I have wanted them to see, they have done so."

"They will go on until they do find them … one way or the other."

Nancy and Grant were questioned whether they would ever leave their home and start afresh.

Nancy: "I can't go in case the kiddies come home. You see, I am waiting for them to come back here. I never know. Perhaps someone could drop them at the front gate. Wouldn't it be dreadful if I were not here?"

9
A Letter from 'Jane'

February 29, 1968

Only one week after *The News* published the extensive interviews given by Nancy and Grant Beaumont, a somewhat cryptic article appeared in the same newspaper regarding a possible break-through into their children's investigation.

The article confirmed that Grant and Nancy Beaumont had recently travelled to Victoria to pursue a new lead, and had stayed in a motel for three days under assumed names.

"It is known they left home before dawn on Sunday to keep a secret rendezvous outside a building in Victoria. In accordance with the lead they were pursuing, Mr Beaumont wore distinctive clothing to make him easily recognisable for any contact which might have been made."

What made this article remarkable was when the journalist tried to explain that the Beaumont parents had travelled to Victoria with a family friend; and *not* a detective!

"Their friend's build could easily have led to the mistaken impression that he was a detective."

The denial that the 'family friend' was a not a distinctive looking detective started immediate speculation. Who was the family friend? And what were the circumstances that led to Grant Beaumont waiting outside a building in a Victorian town dressed in "distinctive clothing"?

Journalist, Alan Dower, in his book 'Deadline' (1977) detailed the extraordinary week in the lives of the Beaumont parents and the 'family friend'.

The story was revealed when journalists, Dick Wordley, Alan Dower, Douglas Steele and photographer Bert Stansbury, were enjoying a schooner of beer (or two) at the Strathmore Hotel, North Terrace, Adelaide; a favourite watering hole for pressmen looking to unwind.

Stansbury, an experience photographer for *The News*, vividly recalled the day he received a call from his chief editor.

Stansbury: "It was a Sunday; early afternoon. My day off, and I was happy enough quietly doing my concreting when suddenly the phone rang. It was John Kroeger, then chief of staff for the News." "Drop everything. Get in here straight away. Bring your camera gear, of course. Bring a razor if you want to. Just drop everything and get in here in half an hour."

Within an hour Stansbury, and fellow photographer Mick Conrey and four other News journalists were heading for the Victorian town of Dandenong, 30 km from Melbourne's CBD, via the Western Highway.

During the long and tedious nine hour trip Kroeger revealed

9 A Letter from 'Jane'

that there had been an extraordinary development in the Beaumont mystery and there was a chance that within 24 hours the Beaumont parents would be reunited with their children.

The posse of newspaper men arrived at their destination around 5 a.m. and by 7 a.m. were staked out around the Dandenong Post Office.

Stansbury: "I'm in a café, about 150 yards from the post office, with my telescopic 'Long Tom', trained on that post office corner like a bazooka with hairline sights. I can't afford to take my eyes off the target for one bloody second in case Jim Beaumont or anyone else pops up."

"It was nearly a couple of hours later… all of a sudden there's a small van there. And a bloke whistling away and wearing working togs. And I can see its Tonner (Stan) Swaine (the head of the South Australian Homicide Squad)."

"All of a sudden I see Jim Beaumont arrive at the corner, and he's dressed just like Kroeger said he would be — dark blue bowling blazer, white pants and so on. And he's waiting there alone and I am clicking madly."

Grant Beaumont found himself 800 km from home, waiting outside the post office in Dandenong because of a letter he received on February 23, 1968. He opened the envelope believing it to be another one of hundreds of letters he had received since the children's disappearance. The contents of which were either, well meaning and sympathetic or of a crackpot nature.

Grant's hands shook as he read the opening line, 'Dear Mum and Dad'. He immediately looked to the bottom of the page. It was from 'Jane' his daughter.

Dear Mum and Dad,

We are safe, so there is no need to worry about us! Oh, we really missed you in the past two years. At the beach on that day, we were walking to the bus stop when a man in a car stopped us and asked us if we wanted a ride. I said that we did and that is how it all started. The man would not let us write before. He is letting us write tonight because he saw the article in the Herald tonight and felt sorry for you both.

He watched us a lot for about six weeks and then he did not watch us so much. Arna and I often talk about you but Grant does not remember you at all after more than two years.

We have been well fed all the time. I as well as Arna and Grant hope that you are both well. The man said to me just now that he will willingly let us go if you will come over to Victoria to get us as long as you do not call the police.

He said that if you do the deal is off. You have to pick us up in front of the Dandenong post office at ten minutes to nine o'clock next Monday twenty sixth of February. You, Dad, have to wear a dark coat and white pants so that the man will know you. The man told me to tell you that the police must not know at all. He said that if you do tell them, you may as well not come, so please do not tell them. The Dandenong post office is in Victoria in case you did not know. We are all looking forward to seeing you next Monday. Please do not tell the police. The man did not mean to harm us. We still love you both.

"Love Jane, Arna and Grant

Grant Beaumont immediately telephoned Stan Swaine the head of the Homicide Squad.

Grant: "I've got a letter from Jane. I want to see you urgently."

9 A Letter from 'Jane'

Swaine rushed to the Beaumont's home. Grant was impatiently waiting on the front porch. After reading the letter a number of times Swaine looked Grant in the eye; "What do you think of it, Jim?" Grant: "It looks like Jane's handwriting."

The letter looked genuine to both Swaine and Grant Beaumont; however the misspelling of Arnna as 'Arna' put some doubt on its authenticity.

Swaine took the letter to Detective-Sergeant Blight, who had been on the case from day one and had kept Jane's school exercise books on file in his office. Swaine and Blight agreed that the handwriting in the letter was similar to Jane's but needed an expert opinion if they were going to take the matter further.

Swaine consulted with C.I.B. Superintendent Lenton, and Johnnie Ramseden was called.

Swaine: "Johnnie then was with the ballistics bureau but had been studying handwriting characteristics for some time. Johnnie had a close look and announced that, although he could not be positive, there were so many similarities which convinced Superintendent Lenton that I should go to Melbourne forthwith, and with utter secrecy I don't know that even the Police Commissioner, Brigadier McKinna, was informed."

At 5 a.m. on Sunday, February 25th, Stan Swaine along with Jim and Nancy Beaumont started their long drive to Dandenong. That night while the Beaumonts were settling into their accommodation Swaine drove to the centre of Dandenong.

Swaine: "I made a thorough reconnaissance of the Dandenong district, kept the location of the police headquarters well in mind in case I needed sudden help, and decided on my course of action for the next day. I borrowed a small, light-colour van.

It was branded 'Hemco Industries' Melbourne. I had a khaki shirt and slacks to pose casually as a window cleaner."

By 7 a.m. the next morning Swaine was incognito — waiting for Grant Beaumont to appear.

Dandenong Post Office

Shortly after 9 a.m. a post office employee, Mrs Alice Parker, was at the front counter registering letters and parcels when the telephone rang.

Parker: "The speaker was a man. The speaker sounded like an Australian. It was masculine and the message sounded genuine."

The caller: "Hello, is that Dandenong Post Office? Look I wonder if you could do me a favour. Can you see a man standing outside your office, wearing white cricket slacks and a blue blazer?"

Parker: "Well, as a matter of fact I can see him from here by looking along the counter and out through the doors."

Caller: "Well would you mind popping out and telling [him] I won't be long? I've had a bit of trouble but I'll be there as quick as I can."

Parker went out onto the footpath where Grant Beaumont was anxiously looking around the busy street.

She relayed the message to Grant and added, "So you won't go away, will you?"

Grant: "No, No! Thank you. I won't".

After delivering the message Mrs Parker returned to her counter. She told her workmates, "You know, that man looks like Mr Beaumont, who had his kids stolen."

Soon after, one of the messenger boys came from the telegram room and told Mrs Parker "I've had a telephone call to tell a man outside that someone will be there shortly."

The boy delivered the message to Grant Beaumont, still pacing up and down the length of the post office's frontage.

Grant Beaumont was being watched closely, not only by Detective Swaine and the Adelaide contingent of *The News*, but also by two journalists from the *Herald* newspaper!

Douglas 'Stainless' Steele, the Chief of Staff at the *Herald* received a phone call early on the Monday morning from a police sergeant at Dandenong. The sergeant told Steele that he had received a call from a local publican. There had been a spate of safe busts in the area at the time and the publican rang to say a stranger had booked in at his pub and wanted him checked out. The local sergeant did the checks and found he was a South Australian detective named Swaine. Steele immediately connected Swaine with the Beaumont case and sent two of his reporters to investigate.

Swaine was doing his best to stay unnoticed and constantly moved his van along the street to allay any suspicion. "I moved the van several times and drove it the long way round the busy block before finding another parking space and getting on with my 'work'. Sometimes I was about four floors up in a building overlooking the post office. Sometimes I was dawdling or pretending to work outside shops in Langhorne Street."

At one stage Swaine approached Grant who whispered: "Grant [Jnr.] is sick and can't be brought until after lunch."

Grant received more messages delivered by employees of two other retail businesses close to the post office. With each message Grant became more agitated.

The waiting continued throughout the day but a short-time after 3 p.m. Grant walked over to Swaine with his balding head bowed and said: "Let's go over to the hotel and talk." Grant Beaumont was all but defeated.

When the two men walked into the Dandenong Hotel, Swaine was shocked to see Adelaide's finest newspaper men staring at him. He was furious that the secret rendezvous had been corrupted. He shouted to the group, "What are you bastards doing here?"

Swaine's outrage slowly dissipated as he, Nancy, Grant and the men from the press drank together for a number of hours to drown their sorrows and frustrations. The highlight of the night was when the Beaumont parents got up to have a dance; they were cheered on by all the hotel patrons.

While the newspaper men returned to Adelaide the following morning, Grant and Nancy stayed in Dandenong for two more days. For both days Grant stood for hours outside the post office waiting for a miracle.

When the Beaumonts returned to their Somerton home, an envelope with the same handwriting as the first letter was waiting in the letter box. Inside were two letters.

Posted February 29th, 1968

Dear Mum and Dad,

We had a really beautiful lunch today. We had some turkey, and a lot of vegetables. They tasted really nice. The man is feeding us really well. The man took us to see the Sound of Music yesterday. Little Grant fell asleep in it though. He could not understand it. The man was very disappointed that you brought all those policemen with you. He knew all the time that they were there; he says that is why he sent the message to go across the street so that it would disturb the positions of the policemen. The man said that I had better stop now, so I will. Grant and Arnna send you their love.

Love Jane, Arnna and Grant.

xxxxxxxxxxxxxxxxxxxxxxxxxxxxx

The second letter was from the 'Man'.

Dear Mr and Mrs Beaumont,

I am terribly sorry that I could not hand you your children back to you when you were in Dandenong, but I knew that you had detectives with you, and the main street was so busy.

I am taking extra good care of the kiddies for you. I took Grant to the doctor because of his gashed knee. He is feeling a lot better now.

Actually in a way, it is your own fault that I did not return them. I saw the letter that Jane wrote before she sent it and it definitely said that there were to be no police (and you know that includes detectives as well).

I apologize also for all the phone calls at the Post Office, William's and Roger David's, but I had to contact you somehow. Like William's the Post Office soon became quite "BITCHY." I got frantic when they would not give you any more messages. Then I got into contact with whom I believe was the Dandenong Post Office Master.

I guess it is too late now, isn't it. I will put them on the train to Adelaide one of these days in the near future, so you had better have their rooms cleaned up!

The assumed Postmaster gave me a phone number to ring. I did so in a hurry. But the girl there lied miserably by saying that a Mr G. A. Beaumont had not been registered there. If only I could have talked to you then, you might have had your children safely by now!

Isn't it a pity you brought those Detectives!

I will write to you as often as possible. I will let Jane and perhaps Arnna write to you.

I am sorry for all the inconvenience I have caused you over the past two and a quarter years (nearly).

Yours faithfully
"THE MAN"

A week later another letter with the distinctive handwriting was delivered to Mr and Mrs Beaumont.

Dear Mum and Dad,
I wish you could have got us when you were over here but the man said that you brought some policemen with you. I wish that you had not done that. If you had not, we might have been home by now with you both. The man said that he will let u come home on the train one day. I want you to now and never forget, no matter what happens that we still love you both very much.
Love,
Jane, Arnna and Grant.
xxxxxxxxxxxxxxxxxxxxx

This was the last letter from 'Jane' and the 'Man'.

10
Dead End

As the 1960s came to an end public interest in the Beaumont mystery declined. Newspapers were now firmly focused on the Vietnam War. Almost 50,000 Australians served in the Vietnam conflict between 1965 and 1972. Many of them were conscripted which split the allegiances of Australians. Towards the end of the decade, tens of thousands of Australians took to the street in mass demonstrations in protests that often became violent.

One of Australia's 'biggest stories' occurred 17 December 1967, when Australia's Prime Minister, Mr Harold Holt went swimming at Cheviot Beach in Victoria. He was never seen again and two days later was officially presumed dead. His remains have never been found.

As time went by police authorities issued an occasional update but the Beaumont case was all but 'dead'. What started out as South Australia's most resourced criminal investigation was eventually scaled back to a single detective.

Although the Beaumont children were definitely not forgotten by the public of South Australia, life in the suburbs of Adelaide slipped back into normality. The scars from this horrible crime were being healed with the soothing balm of time.

Nancy and Grant Beaumont were now alone with their tragedy. Their lives shattered. Nancy had become a shadow of her former self. The attractive, fun loving woman had lost 14 kg, and lived on little more than cups of tea, cigarettes and heavy tranquilisers to get her through the day. Grant battled on with his work but his thoughts were constantly of his children.

While driving through towns as a traveling salesman he would see children and slow down to make sure that one of them was not his own. Everywhere he travelled, in every hotel bar he took refuge in, he was always confronted with the same uninvited questions and theories; the insensitive remarks burned at his soul, but true to his nature he never showed contempt.

The Beaumont case had a brief reawakening in the late 1960s when Victorian Police searched four small islands near Port Phillip Heads. Police dug at a number of locations on what is known as Mud Islands, about 5 km. from Sorrento.

The search began after an anonymous letter to police: "Have you ever thought of looking for the Beaumont children on Mud Islands?" The letter was posted from "Parramatta NSW" and was addressed to the officer in charge of police, at St. Leonards which is 30km east of Geelong.

The four islands were certainly no tourist destination and consisted of 10 acres of barren, dried up muddy earth infested with mutton bird holes and rabbit warrens. The search ended with a predictable outcome; no bodies were found.

In 1968 police once again had another speculative line of inquiry after a tip off that put the spotlight on Port Adelaide's waterfront. A comprehensive police report was prepared on the shipping arrivals and departures at Port Adelaide. One vessel investigators took particular interest in was a ship named 'Devon'. Police became alarmed when they ascertained that not only was the ship in Port Adelaide at the time of the Beaumont's disappearance, but it was also berthed in the Port of Melbourne in 1968 when seven-year-old Linda Stillwell vanished. With help from the Federal Government, South Australian Police managed to stop the ships voyage out of Auckland, New Zealand, on September 19. The crew were questioned about the abduction, finger printed, and individually photographed, but nothing has been said publicly of this matter since.

South Australian Police received an occasional piece of information from the public but nothing of any substance ever came to light. Every lead had been thoroughly investigated; every man that was remotely categorised as a 'person of interest' had been put under extreme scrutiny. There was no crime scene, no tell tale piece of forensic evidence to develop further; no bodies. The police were left 'clueless'.

Police in all States and Territories of Australia as well as New Zealand had chased up every 'tip off'; every 'anonymous phone call' was listened to with intent. Even when police received a speculative theory, it was never completely ignored; in the vain hope it may become a miracle breakthrough.

S.A. Police asked and were given considerable help from Scotland Yard's finest minds, without any positive outcome.

Police organised for the delivery of thousands of flyers delivered to households around the Glenelg and the surrounding suburbs. They printed posters that were sent to every club, school and hotel in South Australia; every police station in Australia had a poster of the lost children; Jane, Arnna and Grant, stuck on its walls.

Police handed out leaflets concerning the disappearance of the children in the languages of German, Italian and Greek.

According to Police the '6ft. surfie' was their only suspect; but who was he? And if he was innocent why had he not come forward to clear his name? Nancy Beaumont was succinct in her belief that there were four people missing; her three children and the man that was seen playing with them.

Newspapers which had initially emblazoned their front pages with sensational headlines of fear regarding the abduction had become more subdued in their view on the tragedy.

The children's disappearance was tidily described as a 'one off'; a 'billion to one chance'; a 'horror story' that could never, ever be repeated …

Jane, Arnna and Grant Beaumont playing in the backyard of their Somerton Park home shortly before their disappearance.

Image courtesy of Today Tonight Adelaide – Seven Network.

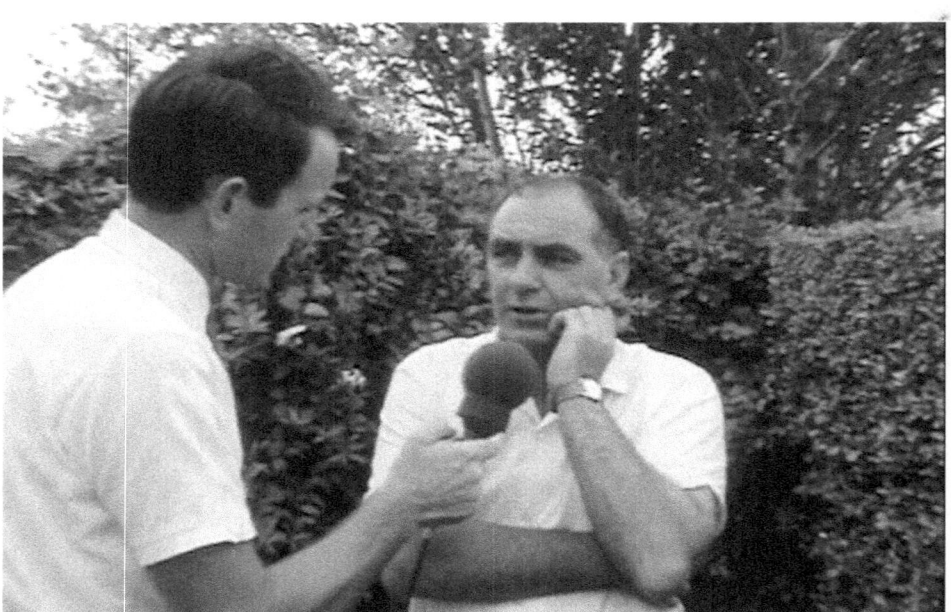

Top: Television reporter Roger Cardwell interviewing Grant Beaumont 24 hours after the children's disappearance.

Bottom: Grant Beaumont leaving his Somerton Park home with Police – January 27, 1966.

Images courtesy of Today Tonight Adelaide – Seven Network.

Top: Crowds of spectators watched on as Police searched the Patawalonga Boat Haven that had been drained. The search began after a witness saw three children matching the description of the Beaumont children near the area on the night of their disappearance.

Below: Cadets from the Fort Largs Police Academy wade through the shallow waters.

Images courtesy of Today Tonight Adelaide – Seven Network.

Police officers and cadets search for signs of the missing children.

Image courtesy of Today Tonight Adelaide – Seven Network.

Members of the public searched along the beaches concentrating on the large storm-water drains.

Image courtesy of Today Tonight Adelaide – Seven Network.

Above: The entrance to the Glenelg Police Station where people gathered waiting to give statements to Police about the Beaumont children's disappearance.

Image courtesy of Today Tonight Adelaide – Seven Network.

Detectives heading the investigation watch on as a rubbish dump is searched for clues to the missing children.

Image courtesy of Today Tonight Adelaide – Seven Network.

In February 1966 a bag and children's swim-wear were found at the Marion dump that were similar to belongings of the Beaumont children. Police cadets spent a week searching the area.

Images courtesy of Today Tonight Adelaide – Seven Network.

Above: Grant and Nancy Beaumont being interviewed by a television reporter.

Below: Television reporter Roger Cardwell stands at the corner of Jetty Road and Moseley Street where the last confirmed sighting of the children was made by postman Tom Patterson.

Images courtesy of Today Tonight Adelaide – Seven Network.

The identikit image of the man seen playing with the children on the morning of their disappearance at Colley Reserve. The image was prepared by a newspaper artist.

Dear Mum and Dad,

We had a really beautiful lunch today. We had some turkey, and a lot of vegetables. They tasted really nice. The man is feeding us really well. The man took us to see the Sound of Music yesterday. Little Grant fell asleep in it though. He could not understand it. The man was very disappointed that you brought all those policemen with you. He knew all the time that they were there, he says that is why he sent the message to go across the street so that it would disturb the positions of the policemen. The man said that I had better stop now, so I will. Grant and Arnna send you their love.

Love Jane, Arnna and Grant
xx xxxxxx xxxxxxxxxxxxxxxxxx xx

On February 23, 1968 Grant Beaumont opened an envelope believing it to be another one of hundreds of letters he had received since the children's disappearance. He was shocked when he realised it was a letter from 'Jane' asking him to travel to Dandenong, Victoria to be reunited with his children. The letter from 'Jane' turned out to be a heartbreaking hoax.

The Beaumont parents in discussion with Police in the backyard of their home.

Images courtesy of Today Tonight Adelaide – Seven Network.

Dutch psychic Gerard Croiset arrived in Adelaide in October 1966 declaring that he would find the children "within two days".

Below: The warehouse where Croiset claimed the children were buried.

Images courtesy of Today Tonight Adelaide – Seven Network.

Top: Detectives and reporters inside the warehouse.

Bottom: Croiset talks to Nancy and Grant Beaumont through an interpreter.

Images courtesy of Today Tonight Adelaide – Seven Network.

In 2006 Seven Network reporter Mike Smithson uncovered archival film of a group of people looking on as police searched for the missing children. When Smithson enlarged the image he was astonished that the tall bespectacled young man, (third from right) was a spitting image of Bevan von Einem. (convicted murderer)

In 2009 the Seven Network programme, *Sunday Night* headed by Ross Coulthart contacted an expert in the field of forensic facial mapping, Kenneth Linge of the UK.

Linge was emphatic with his findings:

"Despite the apparent facial similarity between the two people, some important differences were noted. Therefore in my opinion these images lend no support to the contention that Bevan von Einem is male 2."

Images courtesy of Sunday Night – Seven Network.

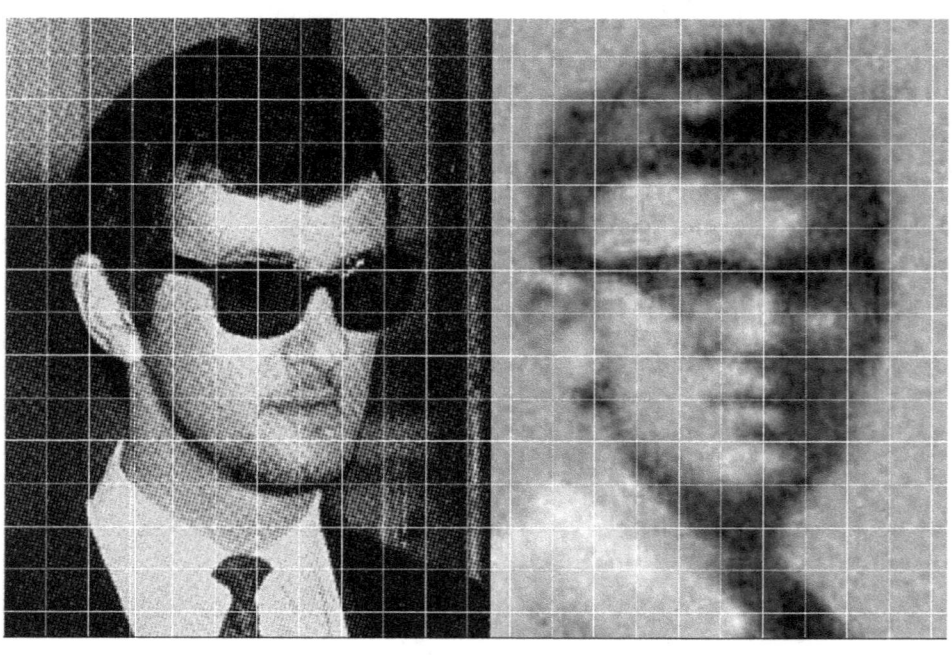

Above: Detectives working on the Beaumont case pictured at Colley Reserve two days after the children's disappearance.

Below: Police officers looking for clues amongst the sand-hills of Glenelg Beach.

Images courtesy of Today Tonight Adelaide – Seven Network.

Image courtesy of Today Tonight Adelaide – Seven Network.

Part Two
"Two Children are Missing"

11
Joanne and Kirste

August 25, 1973

Winter Saturday's were always spent at the footy for the Ratcliffe's; a ritual the family had kept no matter where their beloved Norwood Football Club played or how wet or cold the day was. On this day the Norwood 'Redlegs' were taking on the North Adelaide 'Roosters' at the historic Adelaide Oval; a cricket ground blessed with a serene natural charm.

At 10.30 a.m. Les and Kath Ratcliffe along with their two children, Joanne and David, headed towards the Adelaide CBD, six kilometres away from their Campbelltown home.

Les Ratcliffe parked in his usual place, close to the Torrens River Police Station, 50 metres from Jolley's Boat Ramp; the home of the iconic 'Popeye' tourist boat that cruises along the river.

The children's excitement built as they entered through the

ancient southern gate turnstiles and made their way to the aging but elegant red-bricked Sir Edward Smith Stand.

The Ratcliffe family were greeted warmly by fellow 'Redleg' supporters huddled together on the wooden benches with their red and blue rugs draped over their laps.

Walking through the southern gates of the oval at 11.30 a.m. were Robert (14) and Anthony (13) Kilmartin, ready to start work selling lollies, ice creams and potato chips. The boys had arrived from their Salisbury home (30 kilometres north of the CBD) by train eager to earn pocket money. The boys collected their 'lolly tray' and money bag from the curator's office.

Half way through the preliminary match, Kath Ratcliffe waved to her 'footy friend' Mrs Rita Huckel who was walking up the stairs of the stand with a tiny girl tightly gripping her hand. The toddler was Kirste Gordon her four-year-old grand-daughter. Mrs Huckel and Mrs Ratcliffe had formed a close friendship from their regular meetings at the football, so much so that Joanne referred to Mrs Huckel as 'Aunty Rita'.

Kirste had spent the Friday night staying with her grandparents as her parents Greg and Christine, had decided to take a weekend holiday in the Riverland town of Renmark to catch up with fellow school teacher friends.

All the supporters around the Ratcliffe's made a fuss of little Kirste who was initially painfully shy but Joanne soon made it her business to make the toddler feel more comfortable in an environment which would have been strange to her; there was so much to take in. She looked puzzled at the thousands of people shouting and cheering one minute, followed by the inevitable loud booing and jeering. Joanne squeezed in next to

Kirste and clasped her hand. During the reserves match, the two girls left their seats to obtain straws for their drinks. They returned only minutes later chatting and giggling.

Joanne had clearly taken little Kirste under her wing. Kirste had a head full of beautiful 'honey-blonde' curls and an angelic face which drew attention from everyone. She looked cute, dressed in a white pleated skirt, white tights, brown lace up shoes and a purple jumper. Joanne was a responsible, mature eleven-year-old with a sweet face, sparkling blue eyes and an engaging smile. She was also respectful and obedient to her parents' wishes.

Les Ratcliffe took the safety of his children seriously. He would often brief them on what to do if anything was to go wrong. Les was a caring and protective father who knew the dangers of wandering children. He was proud of the fact that Joanne knew how to dial the emergency number '000' without using coins. He even had rules on when his children could go to the toilet while at the football. Because of the rush of people at the end of each quarter, he was adamant that his children could only go in the middle of the quarters so they would not get disorientated in the crowd and become lost.

The crowd at the oval had grown well past the 12,000 mark.

In the latter part of the third quarter of the league match, at around 3.50 p.m., Kirste became restless and told her grandma that she needed to go to the toilet. Joanne was only too willing to escort her. Lolly seller, Anthony Kilmartin passed the girls as he climbed the stairs; he was hoping to pick up some last minute sales before ending his shift.

The assistant curator of the oval, Ken Wohling, was in the gardener's shed at the back of the Creswell Stand, when he heard children's voices close by. He poked his head through the doorway. He saw Joanne and Kirste crouched down on their knees looking under a parked car trying to entice a kitten out. The motley coloured cat transfixed the two wide eyed girls. "Here kitty kitty, come on… we won't hurt you". Stray cats were plentiful at the oval and children were always trying to play with them.

With the two girls was a man wearing a 'country style' Akubra hat, a grey checked sports jacket and brown trousers. He was of average height with a "stooped" posture. Wohling then heard the man say "I'll try and get them out for you." He then closed the shed's door and returned to his work.

4.01 p.m. Les Ratcliffe stood up from his seat; his face screwed into a frown and looked around for the girls. "They should be back by now". He wandered down to the bottom of the steps and shouted back to his wife that he was going to look for the girls. Les Ratcliffe headed towards the toilets under the Creswell Stand. He felt a little edgy; this was not Joanne's normal behaviour. His steps quickened as he turned into the tunnel — expecting to see the girls playing. He held his breath — the girls were not there. He asked a woman coming from the ladies toilets if she could return to the toilets and check. She did — she shook her head as she came out.

4.09 p.m. The sound of the siren marked the end of the third quarter. Robert Kilmartin sat on a concrete step underneath the Creswell Stand, only metres from the ladies toilet, tired after a busy day. He observed Kirste and Joanne playing nearby with three other children kicking a rubber soccer ball.

11 Joanne and Kirste

During the break in play, crowds of spectators were moving purposely in thick packs in a multiple of directions. A mass of people were spilling onto the lush grass of the oval to hear up-close what the players and coaches were saying; scores of people were also lining up outside the toilets. Men were rushing to the bar under the Creswell Stand for a quick beer.

As was the norm at three-quarter time, the large iron gates of the oval at the southern end of the ground were thrown open to the public for free entry. A dozen or so people walked eagerly through whilst the 'gate staff' busily balanced their money tins.

Anthony Kilmartin, still with his lolly tray weighing on his shoulders noticed two children who he believed were Joanne and Kirste with a man. He watched with interest as the girls seem to be distressed but believed the man chastising them was their father.

The man with a 'country style' hat pulled down to his eyeline had little Kirste wrapped tightly in his left arm with Joanne desperately trying to grab hold of her. Kirste's face was flushed with terror. The man turned towards Joanne and angrily spat out "You little bitch, go away" — "bugger off". In the struggle, a pair of reading glasses fell from the man's jacket pocket onto the ground. As he bent down to recover them, he grabbed hold of Joanne's arm and pulled her along towards the southern gates approximately ten metres away. The wide-eyed lolly boy lost sight of them as they departed through the gates into the car park.

4.17 p.m. The final quarter had begun with the crowd noise building. The temperature began to cool rapidly as the sun receded however Les Ratcliffe perspired heavily as he rushed around the grandstand area, his eyes darting around for any sign of the girls. Distressed, he returned to his wife waiting in the grandstand — he looked towards her — her face was tight and pale. He raced up to her. "Go to the Committee Office — tell them that we need an announcement made on the PA system". He then calmly told his son David to remain in his seat in case the girls came back. "They must be back soon".

Les again ran down the stairs. This time he pushed through the crowd and headed for the concrete players race which was elevated 2 metres off the ground. He stood on it and looked in every direction hoping to see a sign of Joanne and her little friend. All he saw were hundreds of faces focused towards the footy action. "When is that bloody announcement going to be made", he muttered bitterly as he peered up into the Member's area of the grandstand.

Mrs Ratcliffe knocked heavily on the secretary's office door at the top of the stairs. A man appeared. "What can I do for you?"

"Two girls are missing. I need you to make an announcement".

The oval official frowned as he pondered a reply. At first he stared blankly at her. He then asserted his authority, "We can't disturb the game … besides the noise of the crowd would make any announcement useless". He then pointed to the bottom of the grandstand where he told her that two police officers would be there to help her. Watching proceedings from within the office and only a metre away, was a Police Superintendent. The officer in charge for policing the oval kept a deafening silence. Kath Ratcliffe ran precariously down the wooden stairs.

Mrs Ratcliffe felt both despair and anger. There were no

police officers in sight so she and Kirste's grandmother both went searching, leaving young David waiting in hope of the girls returning. "Don't move David, wait for the girls". Rita Huckel suggested that perhaps the girls had left the ground at three-quarter time, thinking that the game had ended. Kathleen Ratcliffe dismissed this theory as Joanne had been going to the football for six years and knew when the game ended. "She would never leave without us".

As each minute passed Les Ratcliffe became more vocal in his search, shouting out his daughters name — "Joanne, Joanne". Spectators glanced at him with mild concern before returning their focus to the action on the field.

Adelaide Oval had a bowling club attached to its perimeter. Les went through every room — asking — pleading "Two girls are missing — have you seen two girls". "The little one has a purple jumper, white skirt". He then ran back to the oval and barged through the green keeper's sheds old wooden door — Mr Wholing looked non-plussed when asked if he had seen the girls. "They are not here." Before Wholing could give a further explanation, Les Ratcliffe had run out.

4.49 p.m. The final siren sounded. A huge cheer came from the crowd. The spectators started to swarm down from the stands towards the gates. Les stood on a small mound near the southern exit as hundreds of people walked past, some with miserable faces of defeat, others cheerful and chatting. "Come on, move on" — Les was desperate for the crowd to disperse so his search could continue — at the same time his eyes scanned the masses of people to catch a glimpse of his precious daughter.

The announcement over the oval's loud-speakers finally came, "Joanne Ratcliffe in Adelaide Oval — come back to your mother and father".

At 5.12 p.m. Les Ratcliffe made a call to the police from a public phone box. Police patrols arrived soon after and began an immediate search of the area.

Into the darkness

As the hours ticked by police put more emergency measures into place. Roadblocks were set up on the outskirts of Adelaide in case the abductor was heading interstate.

All available police vehicles were ordered onto the roads around Adelaide's CBD in the search for the missing girls. Police were not the only people taking part in the search. Les Ratcliffe had rung his former workmates in the taxi industry for help. Before long almost every taxi driver in the Adelaide area was scouting the city streets. Even the RAA (Royal Automobile Association) decided to send all of their bright yellow vans out onto the streets to help with the search.

The city's cinemas displayed messages across the screen alerting customers of the abduction. Early information was vital. Homes around the Adelaide inner city were door knocked throughout the night. Within hours the search had escalated into a massive manhunt. Hundreds of police were involved.

As the news of the missing children filtered into the community, talk of this latest abduction naturally focused on the tragedy at Glenelg Beach seven years earlier. Comments such as "It sounds like the Beaumont children all over again" were being repeated across South Australia. "It must be the same bastard."

The phone rang at the Salisbury home of Det. Sergeant Col Lehmann at 11p.m. He knew it must be important but when he heard the circumstances he was stunned. Lehmann quickly got dressed and sped down the Elizabeth Highway towards Police Headquarters.

Teams of police scoured the murky banks of the River Torrens; a boat with a powerful spot light cruised up and down the river on the lookout for any sign of the girls.

At the oval Lehmann immediately introduced himself to Les Ratcliffe who was now in a deep state of despair. Ratcliffe's eyes were red and swollen, his voice hoarse from crying out the name of his daughter. He broke down as he re-told Lehmann what had transpired that day. Lehmann didn't wait for him to finish. The tall, thickly padded frame of Lehmann towered over the diminutive Ratcliffe; the detective pulled Les closer and let the tormented father sob uncontrollably against his chest.

The hard-as-nails cop patted him on the back as he promised Ratcliffe that every possible resource would be put into place to secure his daughter's return.

Aunty Rita

Mrs Huckel couldn't be consoled back at her home in the inner-city suburb of Mile End; only a ten minute car journey from the oval. Her weeping became hysterical when her husband decided to call Kirste's parents. The Huckel's had been hoping for a phone call from police to say the girls had been found but no such call materialised.

Mr Huckel dialled the number of the Renmark Hotel where the Gordons were staying. As the ringing tones sounded Mr Huckel felt sick — "How do I tell my daughter we don't know where her baby is?"

Greg Gordon (31) answered. He began to tremble as he listened to what was being said but failed to comprehend the true meaning. "Missing, what do you ..." Greg and wife Christine (28) threw their belongings into their car and started the five hour journey home. The two young parents and their baby daughter Catherine had travelled to Renmark to celebrate the 50th Anniversary of the River Murray Caledonian Society. Mr Gordon (a high school teacher specialising in maths and physics) was the Pipe Sergeant of the band during the mid 1960s.

Arriving back in Adelaide at around 3 a.m., Mr Gordon parked the car on the side of the road as there was a police vehicle parked in the driveway. The pain of the journey was etched on their faces as they entered the home. "Is there any news?"

Police worked through the night searching empty warehouses in the city, as well as tramping through the damp parklands that surround the city. Homeless people, sleeping rough were woken and questioned. No one had seen the girls.

August 26 — As the morning light took effect, two large buses loaded with fifty police cadets arrived outside the southern gates of Adelaide Oval. The young men, most still looking like boys, resplendent with their navy blue jackets and matching berets, walked slowly in a line along the grassed areas near the river bank. They then got down on their knees, scouring the grounds and the parklands looking for anything to help the detectives on the case who at this stage were mystified at the lack of sightings since the abduction.

The Police Aqualung Squad were organised into teams of three and began searching the shadowy waters of the River Torrens. While two men dived, the third stood in the shallows and held onto a safety line. The divers were investigating the possibility that perhaps one or both of the girls could have slipped into the river and been unable to get out because of the black mud and thick reeds that lined the river. Strong, icy winds made the search difficult but the specialist team carried on throughout the day, searching over 200 metres downstream. Plenty of rubbish was brought to the surface but nothing was found that could shed light on the case.

Les Ratcliffe returned to Adelaide Oval early on Sunday morning. A small man, who at one time wanted to become a full-time jockey, Les looked understandably dishevelled, as he and Detective Lehmann traced the steps his daughter and Kirste may have taken. He pointed to the deserted Sir Edwin Smith Stand, "We were there, in Row L". He then led Lehmann through the archway under the Creswell Stand into the dark tunnel where the toilets were located. It was a cold morning and as the men walked into the tunnel a sudden chilling breeze gripped them both.

Ratcliffe pulled his jacket tight against his chest and started to recall what he had seen in the area the previous day. He told Lehmann how he rushed around the corner expecting to see the children and how he then asked a woman to check the ladies toilets. Les' speech started to slur. Lehmann saw that his eyes were welling up with tears. Les then became silent. His mouth was open, but words just wouldn't come. The loving father then wept uncontrollably. He tried valiantly to pull himself together, but his voice suddenly became a gasp. His legs gave way and he crumpled to his knees. Lehmann managed to grab hold of his jacket before he hit the ground. He lay motionless on the concrete. Police quickly carried him into a nearby change-room where he was revived.

The *Sunday Mail* newspaper only had a small mention on the front page regarding the missing girls, as the full impact of the disappearance had not made the Saturday night deadline.

Mrs Kilmartin of Salisbury was having breakfast while reading the *Sunday Mail* with her two sons Anthony and Robert when she took note of the brief article describing police searching for two girls who went missing at Adelaide Oval the day before. "Robert, do you know anything about this? Two girls went missing during the footy." Robert shook his head but the younger brother, Anthony, chimed in and told his mum he could remember seeing something odd. Mrs Kilmartin immediately phoned the police.

Anthony Kilmartin told the investigating detectives that he saw a man grab a small girl (Kirste) while a taller girl (Joanne) tried valiantly to rescue Kirste from his grip. He saw the man come from behind a large 'pepper' tree and "swoop" on the two girls. He snatched up Kirste, clasping her under his arm and then struggled with Joanne who kicked him. He retold how the man then grabbed Joanne and dragged her through the southern gates of Adelaide Oval. Kilmartin's description of the man as being, "stooped" and wearing a brown broad brimmed hat, grey check coat and brown trousers — closely resembled that of the man seen by the assistant curator Mr Wohling.

Later that afternoon, Senior Inspector Lehmann told a press conference at the Adelaide CIB headquarters that he was anxious to interview a woman seated on a concrete parapet attached to the Creswell Stand. She was seen near the southern gates a few minutes before the incident with the girls. Police believed the woman, aged about 40, medium build with black hair and wearing a fur type overcoat, may have seen something.

Another lead came forward when a motorist reported that a blue Holden sedan with Victorian number plates was seen on Port Road about 5 a.m. Sunday morning with a young girl in the front seat and another smaller girl in the back.

The next piece of information came from a motorist who spotted two girls matching the descriptions of Joanne and Kirste with a man walking in a westerly direction along Port Road, Thebarton; approximately two kilometres from the ground at around 5.30 p.m. The motorist said the man and the older girl were "fighting".

Police summoned the media to plead for help. "If the person who took the little girls has them hidden somewhere, please let them free unharmed".

Police announced that they would like to talk to a man dressed as a woman who was seen near the women's toilets during the game. The 'man' was described as tall with a protruding jaw and a large nose, wearing a brown pant suit, green shirt, brown wig, silver nail polish, patent leather boots and carrying a hand bag. Police also wanted to talk to a person spotted on North Terrace, Medindie near Scotties Motel at 3 a.m. to come forward. He was also dressed as a woman. The 'whisper campaign' doing the rounds was that a transvestite may have been involved with the abduction.

The 'transvestite' suspicion came to an abrupt halt when a Catholic priest contacted the police and told them that he had received a telephone call from a young man who claimed he was the person seen at Adelaide Oval dressed as a woman. Apparently the man was partaking in a dare with a group of mates from the country on a end of season 'footy trip'. The man told the priest, "It was a joke for a bet which went wrong. Tell the police it is nothing to do with this case, and let them get on with the investigation."

Superintendent Lenton, the chief of the Adelaide CIB emphasised the most important factor in the search was time. "We need help from the public now". "It is no use someone ringing us with the information in a week or even a few days".

Lenton, who was intimately involved with the Beaumont investigation, finished with a statement that everyone in South Australia and beyond were thinking.

"We don't want this to be another Beaumont case".

The media was relentless in their quest for information. Both sets of parents were in shock but accommodated the hungry press in hope that maximum coverage might bring forward fresh information.

Greg and Christine Gordon looked composed but drained as they sat in the lounge room of their home in Hackham West. Sitting on Greg Gordon's lap was a sweet looking blonde girl, Catherine, the two-year-old sister of Kirste. Mr Gordon spoke softly and precisely. "There is not much we can do." "We have to try to keep up a front — if we let our emotions get the best of this, it won't do anyone any good".

11 Joanne and Kirste

Next to Greg sat his wife Christine who dabbed a sodden hanky on her damp eyes. "It might seem to some people that we are trying to remain as detached as possible from all this, but I can assure you it is only a front. It is something we have to do for baby Catherine as well as ourselves."

The Gordon's talked openly about Kirste. Her mother revealed that the four-year-old was extremely shy and would never go off with a stranger. Kirste had only just started kindergarten. "Before that she was even shyer." A sad smile formed on Christine's face as she recalled how Kirste would often hide behind a couch when visitors arrived. At kindergarten Kirste had received highland dancing lessons. After the lessons her proud parents would always question her about what she had learnt. "Kirste was so shy she would run out into the passage to do the dance so we couldn't see what she was doing." The hardened crime reporters looked on in silence at the nightmare the parents were being dragged through.

Later that night, on the other side of town, the small home of Les and Kath Ratcliffe was crammed with friends and family desperately trying to come to grips with this epic tragedy. In the kitchen, Les talked to *Advertiser* reporter, John Doherty. Doherty's pad and pen were nowhere to be seen. He listened to Les' emotional explanation of the last two days; his soft, caring eyes fixed on the contorted face of the tormented father. Les told the reporter that because of Joanne's protective nature she would never run off leaving Kirste. "She would never abandon Kirste. She would fight to protect the little girl."

The two men had met only an hour earlier at Police HQ. Doherty was doing what every good reporter should be doing in such a crisis; hanging around the offices of Homicide detectives, looking for an angle for a story.

As he walked down a corridor, he took a glance through a half opened door. The large frame of Detective Lehmann had an arm around a small figure clad in an oversized lumber-jacket. Doherty stood in the doorway stunned at the raw emotion coming from the cold and depressing looking room. "The jacket was heaving from the sobbing." It was Les. It was the beginning of lasting friendship between the two men. From the outset Les trusted Doherty emphatically and appreciated the sensitive nature of the reporter. Doherty was in awe of this battler's courage.

With the blessing of the Ratcliffe and Gordon families, Police organised a live television broadcast scheduled to begin at 7 p.m. Les Ratcliffe was to front the camera and make a plea for the return of the two missing children. The role of a parent in such situations is to ensure that maximum exposure is given to the case. Police were well aware that with every hour that ticked by without any trace of the abducted children, the chances of finding them alive was diminishing drastically. Police were entering their third day of the search; no leads with any substance had come forward. The family and police were desperate for a breakthrough.

Australians on mass were waiting in their lounge rooms for the 'special broadcast' to begin. Seven years had passed since the nation witnessed a heart-breaking plea from Mr and Mrs Beaumont. In 1966 people were shocked at the crime of the missing Beaumont children; in 1973 the nation were equalled shocked, but also dismayed that a similar abduction could be so brazenly repeated.

Sitting together on a worn linen couch ready to watch the

11 Joanne and Kirste

plea from Les Ratcliffe were a husband and wife who knew intimately the trauma the Ratcliffe and Gordon families were going through. Nancy and Grant Beaumont sat anxiously in their lounge room with Tom Prior, a Melbourne newspaper reporter who had befriended the couple after their tragic loss. The Beaumonts were not at their Somerton Park home but at a newly built unit near the Glenelg waterfront. The grief stricken couple stayed at their home for three years after their children's disappearance in case by some miracle their children found their way back home.

Their unit was small but cosy with photos of their children crowding a wooden cabinet. A kerosene heater glowed in the corner keeping the home warm on a bitterly cold August night.

During dinner Nancy Beaumont talked openly to Prior about their horrendous ordeal. She recalled that the day before her children went missing her son Grant had been happily playing in the backyard, doing what he loved most, making mud pies. As the four-year-old walked back inside he pulled open the door and left his muddy hand-print on the wooden panel of the door. Nancy's voice dropped to a whisper when she revealed to Prior that she never wiped the door clean of the tiny hand-print until the last day before they departed their home to move to their unit. Every day the slowly fading mark of Grant's hand imprint tormented Nancy reminding her of her lost boy. "That was all I had left of him".

The black and white Philips television screen flickered and became a little 'snowy' that night but the grief which creased Mr Ratcliffe's face was clearly visible as he prepared to speak. Prior left his lounge chair and tampered with the antenna; instantly the picture became clear.

Les Ratcliffe in a tired gravelly voice pleaded with the abductor to free the children.

"Drop them on some main street corner".

"I am sure my daughter will do the right thing and go straight to the nearest person she thinks she can trust. If you have any decency in you, and respect for these children, who are only 11 and four, who have never done any harm to anybody whatsoever"...

Ratcliffe's voice went suddenly higher as he looked into the camera as if he was talking directly to his daughter Joanne.

"Your first duty is to protect the little girl with whatever you can. Do not leave her, if possible. If you do, don't go too far away. Go to the first person that you think is a responsible-looking person. I say this because I know you will use your head — keep your head. I have trained you what to do in a situation if these people decide to do this thing to you. I myself will not push for any further investigation. I want you and this little girl back with us. Your mother — she's holding up pretty good. She's got every faith in you... You know we all love you..."

Tom Prior had reported on every possible ghastly crime in his extensive career, but nothing touched him like the disappearance of the Beaumont children. Tears welled in his eyes. He looked over to the distraught couple and could see that Les Ratcliffe's emotional plea had torn at the hearts of Grant and Nancy. Tears flowed down their cheeks. Nothing was said.

When Mr Ratcliffe finished his plea a police officer held up an identikit of the suspect in the Ratcliffe-Gordon case.

Nancy Beaumont wiped her eyes with her petite handkerchief

and then quickly stood up. She pointed at the TV screen, "By gee, they are alike." She was referring to the suspect in her children's disappearance and now the Adelaide Oval girls.

The next day Greg Gordon and his wife Christine were drained to a point of numbness. All day long they had been inundated with phone calls from sympathetic callers, eager to lend support. The same questions of "any news" had to be politely answered with a negative. Detectives in rigid dark suits kept probing questions at the couple, trying to find some sanity in the crime, anything to get the investigation on track, any track.

The answers the Gordons gave were always the same, "No they didn't know anyone who could do such a thing." "No we have no enemies."

As the late winter sun receded Mrs Gordon rested in the lounge comforting her youngest daughter. Greg Gordon and a young reporter from *The Age* newspaper, Ben Hills, were talking quietly together when the phone rang.

Gordon picked up the receiver. "Hello".

A slow, deep voice told Gordon, "I have your daughter".

"What…"

"$25,000".

The caller with a thick Australian drawl demanded a ransom for the return of Kirste.

Mr Gordon, "We want proof that you have our daughter."

The man replied, "Never mind the proof".

"If you want to see your daughter alive I want $25,000 by Thursday."

The phone went dead.

At 6.50 p.m. the phone rang again.

Instantly Mr Gordon recognised the caller with the slow drawl. Gordon called Ben Hills over. Hills listened as the caller once again made his demands. Mrs Gordon grabbed the phone, with hands shaking with rage and with tears washing down her cheeks, pleaded, "If you have our daughter, let me hear her".

The caller hung up.

The mystery caller never made another call. Police believed it to be a hoax.

An empty bed

Alec Mathieson was a senior editor at *The Advertiser*. His career had taken him across the globe. Many a time he had the unenviable task of knocking on the doors of bereaved family members, trying to get them to talk about their recently deceased loved ones. But Mathieson had never found himself in the position of talking to a mother that had just had her young child stolen from her. He obviously wanted a story but was sick in the stomach at the job he had to perform. He gently knocked on the door of the Gordon home in Hackham West. Mrs Gordon answered the door. She held her youngest daughters hand tightly.

Mrs Gordon graciously made the reporter a cup of tea and then slumped onto the couch, still clutching her two-year-olds hand. Mrs Gordon: "We cannot help feeling that she is gone, that we will never see her again".

The young mother said that she and her husband Greg would never give up hope as long as a full scale search was under way for their daughter Kirste and Joanne, "But we dread the day that the police come to our door and tell us that the search is being toned down".

Every night in their three bedroom home, the Gordon's got down on their knees and prayed against all the odds that Kirste would be found.

Mrs Gordon said that if Kirste was dead she would rather know. "I could not bear to think that she was just out anywhere".

"We want her back to take care of her properly".

During the days after Kirste went missing Christine Gordon received stark reminders of her four-year-old daughter. Kirste's presence was everywhere — her pink toothbrush, her toy dolls sitting next to her bed. "I see Kirste's clothes hanging in the closet. If I'm making a cup of tea I see Kirste's 'Skippy' cup and plate in the cupboard. I don't think the full significance of what has happened has really hit us yet. It is all so unbelievable. How can two children vanish without a trace?"

Later that night, Christine Gordon bathed Catherine. Normally both of her little girls would be in the bath playing and laughing.

As Christine carefully lifted her daughter out of the water, she wrapped her in a towel and paused. She hugged her daughter tightly.

Snuggled up in her bed, Catherine was kissed goodnight by her mum.

"Goodnight sweetheart".

As Christine walked away, she heard Catherine's tiny voice.

"Mum, you haven't kissed Kirste goodnight".

Christine looked at her daughter's sweet face and sat down on Kirste's bed and pretended to kiss her missing daughter.

"Thank you mummy".

The two-year-old was missing Kirste badly and the next morning was relentless with her questions regarding her big sister.

"Is she at kindy today"?

"She is just not here at the moment."

"When will she be back?"

Later in the afternoon Catherine became sad, finally realising the reality of her sister's absence.

"Kirste's gone hasn't she mum?"

Within a few months of the abductions Detective Sergeant John Louis McCall was given the lead role in the investigations. McCall, an old-school cop who liked nothing better than finishing a stressful day by downing a few beers and sucking on his 'Camel' cigarettes. McCall had the perfect balance of being well respected within the hierarchy of the police force as well as being admired by his fellow officers. He was also a senior investigator into the missing Beaumont children.

Super Sleuth

The discipline of crime investigation has gradually evolved over the decades but the methodology has remained relatively the same. Crimes back in the 70s were generally solved by following up 'tips' and 'leads' from the general public. A tremendous amount of man hours were spent knocking on doors, taking statements, looking at criminal files packed into ancient metal cabinets. Circa 1973 South Australian Police were still years away from using computers in their workplace. DNA technology was almost two decades into the future and obtaining CCTV vision to nab a criminal was a rare occurrence.

The Ratcliffe/Gordon abduction became the first occasion that a new Scotland Yard investigation system was used by S.A. Police. The system was tagged 'Super Sleuth' but was nothing more than a unique card index filing system. Phone calls were prioritised into three categories. Priority one demanded immediate action, priority two meant that work had to be done but was not extremely urgent, and priority three was to be applied to information which did not require action but was filed for reference only. Taking the calls were mainly junior officers and cadets in their late teens.

What started out as an organised and clinical production line of 'leads' quickly morphed into a 'monster' to administer. At police headquarters, a huge blackboard dominated the special operations room; it had over 200 names written on it. These were 'possible suspects' which needed urgent 'priority checks' to be made on them. The so called 'suspects' were a mixture of known sex deviants, and people who had the finger pointed at them from calls from members of the public.

Newspaper journalists were putting a positive spin on the capabilities of 'Super Sleuth' believing it was keeping the "abduction trail hot".

Sergeant Col Lehmann was convinced the system would solve the mystery of the missing girls. In the first two weeks 3,368 calls had been taken from the public. Seven police officers were engaged full time answering telephones in the early stages of the case.

Where this investigation differs from any previously conducted by the SA Police is that every interview and investigation by a police officer resulted in a standard style report being completed which was then fed into the card index system. No longer could a policeman write "AAC" (All appeared correct) on his report.

Five police cadets worked around the clock on indexing and cross-referencing. After this task was completed, experienced investigators would then take over the system and start referencing and cross-referencing. This was the stage where a suspects alibi might be broken, a name crop up enough times to warrant further investigation, or an incident or a pattern start to become significant.

Scotland Yard detectives who brought the system to South Australia did so under tragic and bizarre circumstances.

One year earlier, Dr George Duncan, an Adelaide University professor drowned in the River Torrens when he was thrown in fully clothed. There was innuendo that the culprits were members of the S.A. Police Force's Vice Squad.

Premier Don Dunstan insisted on bringing in an independent authority to investigate the crime. He commissioned two detectives from London's New Scotland Yard to solve the murder.

Duncan was openly 'gay' and in 1972 homosexuals were regularly targeted along the dark banks of the river's edge. 'Gay bashing' became a regular occurrence; unfortunately it was unlawful to practise homosexuality! Another man, Roger James, was also thrown into the murky Torrens that night. James was walking on a cement path on the edge of the river when he heard a voice from behind him, "Do you give it or take it?" James became terrified and replied "neither". As he turned around he saw a group of men about 30 metres away walking along the path towards him. All of a sudden he saw the men grab a small man and throw him in the water

Dr Duncan had little chance of survival. A non-swimmer, he also was disabled by the fact he only had the use of one lung.

James: "All I saw were hands grasping upwards and just the top of his head. There was no struggle, nothing. And then he just slipped away. It was surreal, it was like it had never happened, if you can understand, it was just like the river swallowed him."

The men then approached James, grasped his arms and hurled him in the river. James landed awkwardly and felt his left ankle snap. With a broken ankle he amazingly still managed to pull himself up out of the water. Laughing men in suits once again pushed him back into the freezing river. One of the men taunted him, "Go save your mate".

At this point one of the men stripped to his underwear and dived into the river to save Duncan who had failed to surface. But Duncan could not be found. James once again pulled himself out of the water in agony and managed to crawl to the top of the bank of the river. He stood at the side the road and flagged down a motorist. A car screeched to a halt and a tall young man helped him into the back seat. The 'Good Samaritan' with the soft, effeminate voice was no other than Bevan Spencer von Einem; in a decade's time he was to be branded one of Australia's most brutal killers.

Mistaken Mystics

In 1974, investigative journalist Dick Wordley contacted Dutchman, Gerard Croiset Jnr., a self proclaimed clairvoyant, artist and touch-healer. Wordley had travelled to Europe in his never ending quest to find children taken illegally from Australia. Whilst in Europe, Wordley interviewed Croiset about the disappearance of the Ratcliffe and Gordon girls. Croiset Jnr. believed Joanne Ratcliffe was buried under a house at Bowmans, 13 km east of Port Wakefield; a tiny settlement 100 kilometres north of Adelaide, which at the time housed a railway station, but not much else.

Croiset Jnr. was the son of possibly the most famous physic of the twentieth century. His father visited Australia in 1966 convinced he could solve Australia's 'Crime of the Century'; the mystery of the Beaumont children.

Croiset visited Australia shortly after the interview and visited the Bowmans area with Wordley and a film crew but nothing was found. Wordley then escorted him to Adelaide Oval. Croiset walked around the oval alone as Wordley watched from a grandstand smoking his usual 'Camel' cigarettes.

Wordley strolled down the stairs in his laconic manner as he spotted Croiset walking slowly in front of the Sir Edwin Smith Stand. "That's where they sat, Row L". The two men walked up the stairs and sat in the same spot that the girls had sat. Croiset fell silent for a number of minutes. Finally he spoke, "I saw the man coming out of the toilet." "He was talking with the girls".

"Come with me". Croiset started walking quickly towards the southern gates. "They went through these gates and headed towards the river ... to play with the ducks".

He said the abductor had followed the children. He explained that the abductor had met the girls and then he and the girls walked around to the Victor Richardson Gates on the eastern side of the oval. "The man and the girls had then gone to a car by the Cross of Sacrifice in Pennington Gardens."

Croiset gave an impromptu press conference outside the southern gates of Adelaide Oval. He told a handful of reporters that the car of the abductor was blue and the man was not wearing a hat as originally thought by police. He went on to say the abductor had been wearing a grey suit with square patterns, a light stripe shirt and a flower pattern tie. Croiset believed the man was now about 42 and weighed about 70 kilograms. He then pointed in the direction of a number of old Adelaide City Council glasshouses situated along War Memorial Drive. "Kirste was strangled in there."

He went onto describe how the abductor had wrapped Kirste in hessian and put her in a box which was later dumped at the Wingfield tip. (A waste disposal dump, 15km from Adelaide's CBD)

Croiset then became animated. He raised his right arm demonstrating how he believed Joanne was struck. He claimed Joanne had been knocked out and left in the boot of the abductors car.

Croiset became silent and ignored the questioning journalists. He walked slowly towards the glass houses. He pointed to a patch of dirt on the western side of the nursery and asked a council worker, "Please dig." "You will find a covered bale and old stones."

The worker called to his colleague to come and help him. They found a shallow pit covered with hay; it was filled with bricks.

Croiset said he had little hope of finding Kirste's body.

"I would have to go to the dump and ... but it's useless".

On the sixth anniversary of his daughter's disappearance Les Ratcliffe stunned an *Advertiser* reporter when he declared, "I have a fair idea of the name of the man who killed my daughter." Disturbingly he also stated that he knew where the bodies of the girls were buried.

Ratcliffe's revelations came from his meetings with a visiting British spiritualist, 60-year-old Doris Stokes. Affectionately known in Great Britain as the 'housewives clairvoyant' she had become a television celebrity with millions of admirers riding on the back of a boom in mysticism which swept the western world in the 1970s. Stokes supposedly had a 'gift' from a very early age and claimed she was prescribed medication to stop her "seeing things". Stokes was in Adelaide as part of a world tour demonstrating her 'powers'. Her popularity was enormous in Australia filling concert halls in every capital city including a number of 'sell out' performances at the Sydney Opera House.

Ratcliffe: "She started by relating quite a good deal of history about our relatives. She said a daughter had 'gone over' and she didn't mention the name Joanne for about three quarters of an hour."

Stokes spoke of the tragedy in a passive voice before she suddenly became silent. Tears started sliding down her cheeks. "She broke down. She started crying. She said she was experiencing Joanne's emotions at seeing Kirste with a man."

Stokes was now wildly animated with her arms flaying about. "She said Joanne was hesitating whether to go back and tell her father or go with Kirste."

Stokes clasped her hands around her throat as if she was being strangled. Les Ratcliffe watched in horror. Stokes was signifying how she believed Joanne had died. "Joanne was being strangled with her necklace."

There were a few minutes of calm before Stokes again spoke. However, her voice was not that of her native Lincolnshire accent but resonated like an Australian child. "Daddy you're too uptight. You can't help me". Les Ratcliffe buried his head in his hands. He believed Joanne was talking to him through Stokes.

In the afternoon, after the meeting, Stokes visited Adelaide Oval to see for herself where the girls had vanished. When she arrived at the oval the winter sun was fading quickly, there was a chilling wind blowing off the nearby Torrens River. Stokes walked silently around the back of the grandstands and then stopped at the pepper tree which the abductor had been seen near.

She then told Les Ratcliffe that she had 'seen' Joanne struggling with the abductor. "Joanne broke free from the man and had tried to lock herself in a small shed in the car park." She said the shed was "linked with tar."

Ratcliffe got excited about the revelation, "I spoke to a workman who told me the shed was originally in the Memorial Drive tennis courts and was cemented in tar".

Stokes then told Ratcliffe a name which she believed was that of the abductor. Ratcliffe was stunned; the name she told him was almost exactly the name that another physic had given him. "Mrs Stokes would only discuss the name on condition that I would take no action and leave it in the hands of the police."

He said Stokes also had told him where the girls were buried. She had guided Ratcliffe to a 'secret' location north of Adelaide. Ratcliffe: "People may think I'm a nut I don't care — I think she and other mediums definitely have something."

Les Ratcliffe had turned to mediums in desperation. Les told a reporter that he and his suffering wife Kath had spent "Every spare penny" on their search for clues to their daughter's disappearance.

His association with mediums had given him an inner calm. Les admitted that he had become constantly aggressive and emotional since the fateful day in August 1973. The mystics had given him a slither of hope. He said that he never sent away anyone who contacted him offering help.

"I'll talk to anyone even Billy the Goose if they think they can help." "My daughter probably gave her life for the other child therefore it is only fair that we leave no stone unturned to find out what happened."

Connected?

The investigations into the Ratcliffe/Gordon abduction and the Beaumont children's disappearance turned out to be carbon copies. Police worked tirelessly on both cases for years without ever having a single strong suspect to concentrate on. Somehow three children disappeared amongst thousands of beach goers and then seven years later two girls vanished in a crowd of 12,000!

The citizens of South Australia rightfully wanted questions answered.

How could two multiple child abductions occur in the same city without any worthwhile clues ever been uncovered?

How could these two tragedies not be connected?

12
Cluster Killings

The Adelaide Oval abduction of Kirste Gordon and Joanne Ratcliffe as well as the missing Beaumont children were priorities for South Australian detectives in the 1970s but unfortunately there were a series of 'cluster killings' that would both defer police resources and shock South Australians to the core.

On February 19, 1977, Adelaide newspapers reported the death of Christopher Worrell (24) in a car accident in the southeast of South Australia, one of 306 fatal road accident victims that year. Worrell was speeding back to Adelaide from a stay in Mount Gambier when his 1969 blue and white Chrysler Valiant blew a tyre making the car roll a number of times killing him instantly. Worrell's lover, James Miller (40) miraculously survived the impact.

Worrell's death possibly saved the lives of numerous Adelaide women as his death ended a killing spree over a two month period that left seven young women murdered. Five were buried in shallow graves in a paddock near Truro, a town 80 km northeast of Adelaide, one at Wingfield, and another at Port Gawler. James Miller was convicted of six counts of murder even though he insisted that he was only Worrell's "chauffeur and mug".

Australia was shocked at the brutal ending of seven innocent lives now referred to as the 'Truro murders'. Commentators began to question what was going on in Adelaide, which had always been known as a stable and conservative minded community. While one shocking cluster of murders had been solved another was about to begin …

On June 24, 1979, Alan Arthur Barnes, (17) was found dead at the South Para Reservoir. He had been murdered and thrown over a bridge. Police reported that he died from loss of blood from his anus which had been ruptured by a 'blunt instrument'.

Two months later on August 28, the remains of Neil Frederick Muir, (25) were found in two garbage bags on the banks of the Port River, Osborne. His body had been cut into pieces and bizarrely, parts of his body had been sewn back together.

There was a three year gap before the mutilated body of Mark Langley, (18) of Paradise, was found near Mount Lofty in March 1982. This was followed by the uncovering of remains of Peter Stogneff, (14) whose charred skeleton was found at Middle Beach on June 23, 1982.

The last murder was that of Richard Kelvin, (15). Kelvin was abducted from the well-to-do suburb of North Adelaide around 6 p.m. on 5 June 1983 and held captive and drugged for five weeks before being murdered. His body was dumped at One Tree Hill, 25 kms North of Adelaide.

Bevan Spencer von Einem was charged and found guilty of Kelvin's murder and was sentenced to life imprisonment.

The Beaumonts lived next door

During the 1980s there was a number of Beaumont related theories that kept the mystery appearing in the newspapers on a regular basis.

In January 1985 an incredible story appeared in the Western Australian newspaper regarding a peculiar claim that the three Beaumont children were alive and had once lived at Reid, a small town, on the W.A./S.A. border.

Mrs Laurel Hill, (56) revealed that her family had lived next door to children matching the description of the Beaumonts in a small railway camp on the Nullarbor Plain. She said a married couple arrived in the summer of 1966 along with two girls and a boy. The parents told the community that the children were fostered.

Mrs Hill: "I am convinced these children who lived next door to us at the camp were the Beaumonts. They matched their description and even wore the panama hats and summer sandals that the Beaumont children were supposed to have worn."

She mentioned her suspicions to other residents in the town but, "They thought I was weird. They didn't believe my story because I am an Aboriginal."

According to Hill, the children were locked away and not allowed to speak with any of the other children. "She would take them to school, take them home during the lunch break and was there again at the end of school. When they got home, they were locked in the yard."

"One day, I found the woman crying. I asked her what was wrong and she said that she had been forced to leave a beautiful mansion in Adelaide."

"When I asked her why, she said that because of what he (the woman's husband) had done in Adelaide, they could never go back to their home. She said she would never forgive him."

Police interviewed Reg and Laurel Hill, who said they had lived next door to the suspect couple for nine months from March 1966. Mr Hill described the husband as around 45 to 50 years-old, suntanned, with fair hair, who worked as a linesman. His wife looked older and worked as the postmistress.

Not surprisingly, it turned out that the Hill's version of events were based on vivid imaginations.

The couple at the centre of the allegations were eventually tracked down and interviewed. It didn't take long for the detectives to confirm that the three children were indeed their own and cleared of any suspicion.

The woman told the media, "My husband and I went to Reid with our three children in 1966. Our children were Helen, 9, Catherine, 8, and Mark, 4."

The idea that the Beaumont children were still alive and that they had been snatched and taken to a remote location without being physically harmed was not as speculative as you might think.

In 1976, four-year-old Peggy Clements was abducted from her parent's vehicle outside the Cobar RSL, NSW. Her mother had entered the club to look for her husband. She parked the utility outside the front door and ran inside leaving Peggy with her other daughter.

Her husband told her he had to finish a game of snooker and would be out in a few minutes.

She returned to the car and waited for another 20 minutes until she decided to go back into the club.

"I locked Peggy and Zannette in the front seat because I didn't want them running on to the street and getting hurt."

"I was gone for just three minutes."

Kenneth Charles Stuart, a 46-year-old truck driver abducted Peggy and was later arrested in South Australia on his way back to his home in Marble Bar, Western Australia.

During the trial when he was asked about the identity of the child, later identified as Peggy Clements, Stuart replied: "That's Helen. She is my daughter. She looked like my daughter. She had a scar on her head like my daughter."

"I had to take her because I wanted to keep her … I wanted to bring her up. If your had not found me I would never have given her back."

"Bizarre find"

In March 1986 there was a discovery of an extensive file of newspaper clippings regarding the Beaumont investigation at the West Torrens council rubbish dump, which renewed interest in the ongoing saga. The rubbish dump is at the end of Morphett Road, about three kilometres from the Glenelg beach.

Six Major Crime Squad detectives and a team of technical service police worked through the night sifting through bundles of papers found in three suitcases by council workers. Almost every one of the newspaper cuttings had cryptic annotations written on them in a distinctive red ink.

One newspaper, dated August 5, 1966, had a headline: 'Beaumont children: People hunt in sand-hills.' Scrawled across the page in red were the words "Not in sand hills, in sewerage drain." The same cutting also contained a photograph of the children; written over the image of Jane was an inscription: "She used to comb my hair."

Another 1966 article referred to Mrs Beaumont's belief that her children were alive; written across the top were the words: "No, No, No."

A newspaper clipping that quoted Mrs Beaumont as saying "Someone has got my children," the mystery writer has added: "Did have". Another cutting featured a photo-fit image of a man sought by police in connection with the children's disappearance. Written over the picture was: "Lies — all bluff."

Written across a 1971 report that the children were still alive are the words: "Ha Ha. What a laugh, Big deal."

A few days after the initial find, family members of a recently deceased relative came forward to police and admitted to dumping the suitcases with the newspaper clippings after clearing out the elderly woman's home. The woman was described as "eccentric".

New claim from girl

In March 1988 an Adelaide woman came forward with a claim she had evidence which might solve the tragic mystery of the Beaumont children.

The woman said that as a 10-year-old girl she met and played with the three Beaumont children on the day they disappeared.

She recalled playing with Jane Beaumont throughout the afternoon — until a man came to collect the sisters and their brother.

In an interview with the *New Idea* magazine, the woman said she could remember seeing a man standing behind the seawall at Glenelg. She said Jane Beaumont had pointed at the man and said they had to go with him.

The woman stated that she clearly remembers what the man looked like and what he was wearing and claims the children had collected their things and left the beach quite happily with the man.

The woman says she has been tormented for most of her adult life, knowing she might have been able to help find the children.

"But over the years, every time I mentioned it my family tried to shut me up. As a result I don't get on very well with my family anymore".

"I was watching television at my godmother's house when their photographs came on the news. I recognised them straight away as the new friends I'd made at the beach. I knew something had to be very wrong about them going away, but I really didn't understand it all and when I told my godmother about it she told me it was none of my business."

Russian woman may hold key

In February 1989 an anonymous letter to the Brisbane Homicide Squad claimed the man responsible for the abduction of the Beaumont children was the same person who grabbed a girl off a Greenslopes (Brisbane suburb) street on November 27, 1963.

The police believed that the man who abducted the two-year-old girl in Holland Street, around the corner from Henzell Terrace, lived in one of the flatettes. Despite a huge police search he was never located. New information received in the letter suggested he had fled to Adelaide.

A Police spokesman, Det. Sgt. Nikola, stated that "We have now come to the stage where we need to trace the Russian woman and anyone who lived in Henzel Terrace, in the early 60s".

Back in 1963 a Russian woman told *The Courier-Mail* that the man was an "unwanted friend" of hers, and occasionally drank methylated spirits.

Det. Sgt. Nikola, "We especially want to hear from people who lived in even-numbered houses in Henzell Terrace or near the old Queenslander in the street which, in those days, had eight flats in it." "If we can trace her [Russian woman] or one of the former occupants of the flatettes, we may hopefully get a name — and even a photo — of the man".

The man who wrote the letter said he came forward after reading a recent article about the Beaumont case in a women's magazine.

He said he had also recently seen an old identikit picture of the Adelaide suspect and believed it was the same person he had seen at a football game while on a visit to Adelaide.

His letter stated:

"The man was cleaning up the oval grounds, picking up papers, with a spear prong. My eyes locked on his face. I instantly recognised him as the man wanted nearly 20 years before in Greenslopes."

"He seemed stunned for a moment then he quickly was lost in the crowd."

The newsworthy stories regarding the Beaumont case during the 1980s paled into significance when in March 1990 a witness came forward that would forever change people's understanding on the mystery.

13

'Von Evil'

March 17, 1990

The sensational headline, "VON EINEM KILLED TEN" which featured boldly on the front page of the Adelaide *Advertiser* wasn't a total surprise for most South Australians. Bevan Spencer von Einem was a convicted deviant killer, however the information that followed was simply spine tingling.

During a committal hearing where von Einem was charged with the murders of Alan Barnes and Mark Langley, a crown witness, known as Mr B, told the court hearing that von Einem had admitted to him that he had murdered at least 10 people including the Beaumont children, Joanne Ratcliffe and Kirste Gordon!

Mr B claimed that von Einem revealed to him that he had abducted the Beaumont children, and then "connected them up" and "did some brilliant surgery on them".

He then asserted that the bodies had been dumped at either

Moana or Myponga; both locations south of Adelaide.

Mr B further alleged von Einem had told him he had "picked up two children at the football." Police assumed that "at the football" was a reference to the disappearance of Joanne Ratcliffe and Kirste Gordon at Adelaide Oval in 1973.

Even though Mr B helped police with their investigations, he was certainly no 'angel'. He and von Einem had regularly picked up young, male hitch-hikers before drugging and sexually assaulting them. Often the victims were then delivered to a Henley Beach Road home of three 'drag queens', where they would again be sexually assaulted while comatose by drugs.

Mr B alleged that at one time he entered von Einem's bedroom and found him with a naked, semi-conscious youth. Mr B noticed that a torch and a type of "crochet hook" were both inserted deep into the boy's anus. He said he had also seen items like stainless steel egg cup caps in von Einem's room which von Einem allegedly told him he used for doing circumcisions.

Mr B said he wasn't happy with the practice of picking up youths and drugging them, but had gone along with it because von Einem had supplied him with copious amounts of drugs and alcohol.

Mr B: "I was only 22 at the time. I could relate to people younger than him better." Mr B said he did not have a sexual relationship with von Einem because he found him "repulsive". But he admitted von Einem had said he found Mr B "cute, sexy, nice" and he liked (Mr B) sexually. He said von Einem had frequently referred to enjoying "doing a bit of surgery" on males he found attractive.

He believed von Einem had been responsible for five murders between 1979 and 1983 which have become known as the 'Family Murders' and included Barnes and Langley.

From 1979 to 1983, five boys and young men were abducted from the streets of Adelaide, sexually assaulted and brutally murdered. However, it was the method of their deaths that was so disturbing. The common theme was surgical mutilation; the 'signature' to these murders were the horrific anal injuries.

Von Einem grew up in a quaint cottage in the inner-city suburb of Gilberton with his sister and brother. His father, a self-employed painter and decorator, served in the RAAF in various bases in South Australia during the Second World War. His mother was a gentle, subservient soul, who doted on Bevan as a child. Overly protective of her timid son, she realised from his early teenage years that Bevan was different. He refused to participate in sport and found it difficult making friends with peers, preferring the company of adults. Von Einem was educated at Pulteney Grammar, a prestigious boys' school situated on the edge of the South Terrace parklands, home to the infamous Veal Gardens which for decades was known as a prolific paedophile meeting area.

Von Einem was not a popular student at school and was often teased because of his effeminate ways. He became reclusive and secretive as a teenager and aloof with anybody but his direct family. His favourite activities were reading, practicing on his exquisite-looking golden harp, as well as being an enthusiastic member of the Pulteney Boys Choir.

After high school, he studied bookkeeping and became a qualified accountant during the mid 1970s. He spent most of his working life employed by Pipeline Supplies, which was situated in the heavily-industrialised area of Regency Park.

Von Einem was sentenced in November 1984 to life impris-

13 'Von Evil'

onment with a record non-parole period of thirty-six years for the murder of Richard Kelvin, the fifteen-year-old son of the then Channel Nine newsreader, Rob Kelvin. Kelvin died from a loss of blood due to anal injuries. The revelation that Kelvin had been held captive for a number of weeks had always puzzled police. It simply was impossible Kelvin could have been held in von Einem's home for that period of time without anybody becoming aware of it as he lived with his mother; it was obvious von Einem had accomplices.

Police at one time speculated that there were up to twelve members of a 'family' of like-minded deviants who abducted boys and young men, however von Einem is the only one serving prison time for the crimes. Three other suspects have been identified by police, but their names have been suppressed by court orders.

Myponga

South Australian Police began searching Myponga Reservoir, situated on the Fleurieu Peninsula in early 1990 following a statement from Mr B given to Sydney police in September 1989 that implicated von Einem in the disappearance of the Beaumont children and Ratcliffe and Gordon from Adelaide Oval.

Situated approximately 60 km from the city of Adelaide, the construction of Myponga Reservoir was completed in 1962 and is spread over an area of 3 square kilometres, once known as 'Lovely Valley'. The 226 metre long reservoir wall (which had a road crossing) is approximately 50 metres in height. For a number of years, cars were allowed to drive from one side of the reservoir to the other. There were rumours that the abducted children had been thrown from the dam wall into the water below.

Police divers began searching the reservoir on 2 February 1990. The official police media release stated that they were searching for a strongbox and stolen goods.

Within a few days speculation was rampant that the search was for the remains of the Beaumont children. Police then admitted the divers were searching the Myponga Dam for "bodies" but would not reveal any further details.

A second search of the reservoir began in late February, with police still refusing to confirm that the search was for the remains of the missing children. However when the sensational news regarding Mr B's testimony was allowed to be published in mid March 1990, police finally confirmed that their search of Myponga Reservoir was regarding the disappearance of the Beaumont children.

Grant Beaumont talks after 22 years

Grant Beaumont was visited by an *Advertiser* reporter to get his views on Mr B's allegations regarding the connection between von Einem and the disappearance of his children.

Ever since Mr B first linked Bevan von Einem to the Beaumont case, Grant Beaumont had reporters from across Australia pestering him day and night with unwanted phone calls. Grant would answer the calls but pretend he was a friend; he would politely tell them, "Mr Beaumont isn't in".

Grant Beaumont was non-committal when asked if he thought the evidence given by Mr B meant the mystery of his children's disappearance was getting closer to being solved.

"I don't know what to believe, I don't know any more than you".

Grant Beaumont explained to the *Advertiser* reporter that he wasn't well and had been treated by his doctor for a stress related illness after *The News* printed an article which purported to be the first interview with him for 22 years.

Grant: "I was conned".

The *News* reporter, Leon Bignell, was young and energetic with a touch of brashness when he knocked on the front door of Grant Beaumont's Glenelg home in early 1990. Like many before him, Bignell was hoping for an 'exclusive'.

When Grant opened the door he told Bignell that he was a 'friend' of Mr Beaumont and was doing some cleaning while he was away.

"Jim isn't here and even if he was he wouldn't want to talk to you".

"In fact I won't even tell him you called because it would upset him too much."

Bignell knew he was being outsmarted and made an embarrassing retreat.

However six weeks later he came back with support.

Bignell brought with him the *News* pictorial editor, Bert Stansbury. Bert was once an ace photographer for the *News* and was assigned to the Beaumont case in the early days of the children's disappearance. He and Grant Beaumont also spent time together, in the infamous 'Dandenong trip' in 1968, when police and a pack of journalists from *The News* travelled to the town to hopefully see the Beaumont parents reunited with their children.

After so many years, Grant Beaumont didn't immediately recognise Bert but the two quickly conversed about the 'old days', however Grant became understandably guarded when the subject turned to his children.

"I don't talk about that anymore. That was 24 years ago."

"I want to get on with my life."

"I won't be satisfied until the police bring me something, some sort of evidence."

"Even if a newspaper or a magazine offered me $100,000 for my story I wouldn't sell it. The only thing I am interested in is if someone can tell me what happened to my children."

Bignell revealed in his article that Grant Beaumont had only agreed to tell his story so that it would stop the constant calls.

"I have had to deal with idiots with crystal balls for years and years."

"The hard part was that normally rational people were believing what these people had to say."

"They were clutching at straws in the hope one of these people could solve the case."

Grant Beaumont discussed the frustration of not being allowed to be left alone while going about his normal day to day living.

"I go into a pub and see people staring at me and you know they are talking about you."

"Some idiots with three or four drinks in them come over and say: 'You're the father of the missing kids.'"

"They say they feel sorry for you and all that and go and on."

"I don't want that. I just want to be left alone."

"I am very happy with my lifestyle — except my name is still Beaumont and I'm not going to change that."

"It is unbelievable what some people think and say. One even thought I did it myself."

Nancy Beaumont was also contacted but had little to add regarding the von Einem connection; "I know as much now as I did then."

"I have never heard of anyone coming back from the dead. So maybe we will never know."

14
"I Found Jane Beaumont"

In 1960s police forensics was in its infancy, however by the early 1990s forensic technology had made fighting crime a lot more scientific. 'Cold cases' were given a new lease of life.

'The letters' from 'Jane' and the 'Dandenong Man' were the only material pieces of evidence available to police. When the letters were forensically tested back in 1968 no clues to the identification of the author could be ascertained.

However, in early 1991 South Australian Police informed the public that they had once again reopened investigations into the missing Beaumont children as the result of advancement in forensic technology.

"With these advances in technology now available to investigators we are able to take some lines of investigation a little further than was previously possible."

Major Crime Task Force detectives had travelled to Victoria and questioned a Melbourne man, 41, and obtained a sample of his handwriting, as well as his finger print sample for further testing back in Adelaide.

After exhaustive analysis it was confirmed the fingerprints found on the letters and the handwriting were that of the Melbourne man, who would have been 17-years-old at the time of the 'Dandenong letters' saga that callously raised the hopes of the Beaumont parents.

Surprisingly SAPOL stated that the Melbourne man would not face any charges owing to the limitation of time statutes. Police explained that the man wrote the letters as a "hoax" and they were "In no way connected with the disappearance of the three children."

According to a SAPOL spokesman, "The person involved is extremely remorseful and it would seem that an act he has carried out as an immature young person has come back to haunt him."

Former Homicide Squad detective Stan Swaine, who was in charge of the Beaumont investigation from 1967, summed up the situation adeptly, "Thank God it has been cleared up. We are back to square one".

Six years later Stan Swaine's name was back on the front page with an incredible claim regarding the disappearance of the Beaumont children.

Swaine came forward and asserted he had "found Jane Beaumont".

South Australian Police were naturally interested in this new revelation but were sceptical of its origins. Not that the police doubted Swaine's detection skills; he had proven to be a capable detective while in the force, however since leaving the police force to become a private detective he clearly had become 'speculative' with his theories regarding the Beaumont mystery. Some said he had become obsessive with solving the crime.

Stanley 'Tonner' Swaine was unashamedly different. A man who enjoyed many varied interests away from the disciplined regime of the police force, Swaine quickly rose through the ranks because of his dogged perseverance in combating crime.

As a traffic cop in 1952 he was involved in an incident that would change his life forever. Swaine and his partner (Raymond Morros) gave chase to a motorcyclist along Henley Beach Road and signalled the rider to stop. The rider, James Turner, finally pulled over to the side of the road and stood by his machine and waited menacingly for the officers to approach him. As Swaine walked towards Turner he noticed that Turner had what looked like a screw driver in his hand.

Swaine: "What's the matter with you?"

Turner suddenly lunged at Swaine and stabbed the officer twice in the head. The first blow split open the centre of Swaine's forehead; the second slashed deeply into his eyebrow. Swaine reeled back from the savage blow, with blood spouting from his wounds. Blood instantly covered his face.

Morros who had crept behind a truck parked in front of Turner's motor cycle dived on Turner and a violent struggle began. Significantly blinded, Swaine drew his pistol and shouted "Drop it, drop it".

In fear of his partner being fatally wounded, Swaine aimed his pistol at Turner's hand and fired. The bullet missed its target and pierced Turner's heart.

During the Coroner's Inquiry into Turner's death it was revealed that Turner, a gold fossicker of Mount Compass, had a history of mental illness and that he may have thought the policemen were going to take him back to the Glenside mental health institution. Another theory put forward was that Turner had deliberately set out to murder a police officer that day.

In 1958 Swaine became a founding member of the Anti-Larrikin Squad; a team of policemen appointed to stamp out trouble in the city. Much of the squad's early work involved breaking up gangs of "Bodgies and Widgies" who gathered in Rundle Street (now Rundle Mall).

Swaine suffered from his injuries all his life with debilitating frontal lobe headaches and many bouts of blurred vision.

While recuperating from his injuries he sought advice from another police officer who had become adept at hypnotism. Swaine, a charismatic man, took to hypnosis with enthusiasm and held a number of seminars around Adelaide promoting the benefits that could be obtained from this ancient practice.

Swaine was always looked upon by the Police hierarchy as someone with leadership qualities and was rewarded with a secondment to London's Scotland Yard to study their latest detection methods.

It was while in London that he thought he had hit the jackpot. Swaine dabbled in 'penny dreadful' stock market shares and had purchased shares in Poseidon, a small nickel prospector. The shares started to skyrocket; Swaine was about to become wealthy when the truth of a 'mammoth nickel find' was uncovered and forced the shares to drop like a stone. Like many of his fellow shareholders, he held onto them until they became worthless.

Swaine's sensational claim that he had found Jane Beaumont in a Canberra suburb was not going to plan. The 41-year-old woman in question, who was referred to as 'Susan', wasn't keen to come forward and attempted to have a restraining order issued against Swaine in Canberra's Magistrates Court.

Swaine (72) shuffled out of the court house with the aid of a walking stick but he still looked an imposing figure (190cm) when confronted by the crowd of journalists that waited outside the court. Undeterred by the media attention he told an *Advertiser* reporter that he would not rest until he proved to the "knockers" that he could solve the case. He then claimed that 'Jane' may have been a member of a satanic cult and after suffering amnesia for a number of years had "only realised recently that she could be Jane Beaumont."

The former chief of the South Australia Homicide Squad revealed that he had met the woman on several occasions and that she had shared many of Jane Beaumont's characteristics including the same birth date — September 10, 1956.

The following day Swaine once again claimed front page headlines with a peculiar allegation that the Beaumont children were handed over to a cult.

"I think there is evidence that somehow or other they were handed to somebody. It's my opinion, on the weight of the evidence that I have detected, they weren't abducted."

"The girl told me herself that they were handed over to a cult."

S.A. Police Assistant Commissioner, Rob Lean, issued a statement declaring that detectives would speak to Swaine and the mystery woman and vowed that the information would be thoroughly pursued, including fingerprint and DNA testing, "even though several other leads Mr Swaine had investigated in recent year had all proved fruitless."

According to Swaine the mystery woman had first approached him. "She sent me her address and, in fact, I have met her and spent quite a bit of time with her one day. I've reached the point that all the information I've got on this person is that there are lots of things to indicate that she may well be this person (Jane Beaumont)."

During an interview with Swaine, 'Susan' claimed to also know the whereabouts of Grant Beaumont but never elaborated on her story.

'Susan' in fact had initially contacted the *Woman's Day* magazine 18 months previously and claimed to be a missing 'Beaumont'. Swaine was then contacted by the magazine to investigate her claim. The woman made the claims after attending sessions with a Canberra therapist, who she started visiting after she apparently suffered trauma caused by witnessing an attempted murder.

The former detective was adamant he wanted 'Susan' to undergo fingerprint testing. "There's only one fact that would prove who she is and I understand that would be fingerprints available off [Jane Beaumont's] schoolbooks."

Swaine believed he had support at the highest level. "I'd like to state this ... I have been in liaison with a ranking officer in the SA Police; I'm not just out on a limb doing this. I think I'm pretty level-headed and factual. I'm only telling you what I know as an investigator and I'm free to be queried."

Within a week of the Swaine's allegation, S.A. Police had dismissed the claim that the mystery Canberra woman was Jane Beaumont after finding their birth dates did not match. The woman's birth date differed by about a year from that of Jane Beaumont, which police believe precluded the need for fingerprint or DNA checks. However there was more intrigue when it was revealed 'Susan's' birth certificate was only formally issued in 1966 but this peculiarity was clearly explained by her parents.

The Police's focus immediately turned to the welfare of 'Susan', who they believed to be mentally ill. It was reported that she had no friends and had taken out restraining orders against several Canberra people including her former therapist. It was reported that at a recent court hearing Susan had locked herself in a courtroom and caused damage.

Although Stanley Swaine was devastated by the news his investigation into the disappearance of the Beaumont children had once again turned to naught, he stood firm on his views on where the investigation should head.

"There's never been an official body to examine all facts, like a royal commission type of situation. "It haunts me. I'm disappointed. That's it. What more can I say."

Canine Detectives

The 30th Anniversary of the 1966 Australia Day mystery was only a month away when news broke that the infamous warehouse where Gerald Croiset believed the Beaumont children were buried would be once again excavated.

John Schouten the manager of the warehouse back in 1966 believed that the original excavation had been executed in the wrong area.

Once again, Con Polites, the wealthy property tycoon was

eager to help finance a thorough dig of the warehouse. Polites was willing to import a ground-penetrating radar device to try to locate any remains.

Polites explained: "If we find the children, then we'll solve the mystery. If we don't find them then I'll be very happy because at least we tried and the children could be alive and living somewhere else."

Frank Church, a private investigator was contracted by Polites to track down the children who had once played at the warehouse. It had been reported back in 1966 that Jane and Arnna had played in the disused building with friends from the Wilton Avenue area.

In March 1996 Polites met and spoke with a 38-year-old man who as a child had played at the site of the old brickworks. The man pointed out a series of tunnels fanning out from the main area excavated in 1967.

After thorough research, private investigator Frank Church summarised what he believed was under the concrete floor.

"Where the underground tunnel was situated was at the base of a huge machine. A pit had been dug to let employees get to controls at the base. The local kids could get in there and they had dug a sort of cave but it never went back into the wall more than two feet and if it had collapsed would have been noticed the following day by the workers."

On April 30, 15 holes were dug into the floor of the warehouse. Two appeared to have been filled with gravel and sand and samples of these were taken for examination by Geraldine Hodgson, a forensic geologist. Drilling began again the next morning, but nothing was found except a second layer of concrete.

Two weeks after the dig began Polites announced that "No organic evidence of human remains was found in recent drill samples."

On the weekend of 23-24 June, two cadaver dogs trained by Janet Crease were brought to the excavation site. Crease and her Weimaraner dogs had been successful in N.S.W. in tracking down lost people in bushland as well as being used by investigators into suspicious property fires. (Crease was the first person in Australia to train and use dogs for accelerant detection.)

Once the two 'canine detectives' were carefully lowered into the deep pit they became agitated and started digging furiously at the western side of the pit. Men with picks and shovels then concentrated their digging in this area but nothing was found.

The digging was put on hold for two months and resumed in early September. The closest the excavation came to finding anything was when a 13cm bone was uncovered. Forensic tests established that it wasn't human.

The excavation of the warehouse ended with no human remains discovered although the excavation was not a total waste of time as it finally put to rest, once and for all, the notion that the children somehow were accidently buried.

15

Persons of Interest

South Australian Police have never come out and publicly named a suspect in the Beaumont abduction but over the last 50 years there have been many investigations into 'persons of interest'.

In August 2007, SAPOL became aware of archival television footage which would once again attach the name of South Australia's most notorious convicted killer to the missing Beaumont children.

'Von Evil'

Bevan Spencer von Einem, South Australia's most reviled murderer was the person in question. A young man baring a remarkable likeness to von Einem, (who would have been aged 20 at the time), was seen watching police divers search a drain at Glenelg a few days after the children's disappearance.

The television footage was uncovered by Mike Smithson, a

reporter for the Seven Network. He was trawling through archival film looking for images to use in a television story when he stumbled on a group of people looking on as police searched for the missing children. When Smithson enlarged the image he was astonished when he realised that the tall bespectacled young man, was a spitting image of von Einem. The man had jet-black hair which fitted von Einem's appearance at the time. Von Einem's hair had dramatically turned to silver grey in his late teens which he then dyed black on a regular basis.

Smithson's 'find' was shown on national television and led to SAPOL detectives becoming involved.

As previously stated, von Einem was convicted of the murder of fifteen-year-old Richard Kelvin in 1983 but there has always been widespread speculation that he may have been involved with the killing of four other young men in the late 1970s and early 1980s in what has become known as the Family Murders.

Von Einem was first linked to the Beaumonts in 1990, when he was facing charges of murder in regard to two other Family Murder victims. As previously stated, at the committal hearing a witness, known as Mr B, told the court von Einem had admitted to him that he had murdered the Beaumont children.

Was von Einem returning to the 'scene of the crime'?

Returning to the scene of the crime

The idea that a killer returns to 'the scene of the crime' is not just a plot development used by television script writers.

The concept is backed by research from the Federal Bureau of Investigations (FBI). A FBI report in 1999 suggested that in

27% of murders, the killer returned to the crime scene albeit with many weird and varied reasons: 26% stated that they returned to relive the fantasy of the murder; 19% to check on the police progress of the crime; 9% to kill another victim; and 6% to have sex with the corpse.

The FBI discovered another remarkable aspect of what they termed the 'totem phase': In 20% of the homicides they had studied, the killer actually participated to some degree in the police investigation of the crime.

"In cases of children going missing, the killer is often among the volunteers looking for the missing child."

The "FBI Crime Classification Manual" (Douglas, Burgess, Burgess and Ressler) revealed that murderers are roughly divided into three categories: organized, disorganised and mixed.

An excerpt from the book suggests that, "Because of afterthoughts, like regrets or fear to be discovered, the disorganized serial killers can return to the crime scene, hiding in the crowd."

John Douglas, one of the FBI's premier profilers, backs up the findings. "This stuff has been around for years, the subject returning to the scene of the crime. That's the kind of thing Sherlock Holmes did. We just verified it. Not just serial killers but arsonists and bombers go back to see their handiwork. This is their accomplishment… He is driven to go back."

Von Einem was questioned over the disappearance of the Beaumont children and he gave a brief statement to police while waiting in the cells of the Adelaide Magistrates Court prior to his appearance on child pornography charges. However, speculation regarding von Einem at the 'scene of the crime' was quickly snuffed out when Major Crime Superintendent, Tony Crameri, declared, "There has been no evidence produced which furthers this line of inquiry and it is now complete."

One month after SAPOL began looking closely at the 'von Einem' lookalike, Nigel Hunt of the *Sunday Mail* dropped a bombshell when he claimed that a confidential police report prepared in 1989 by the Major Crime Squad, linked von Einem to the disappearance of the Beaumont children and Joanne Ratcliffe and Kirste Gordon.

The 1989 police report triggered various police investigations that examined the similarities between the two abduction cases. One inquiry focused on von Einem's known involvement in the drugging and sexual assault of young male victims as well as von Einem's residential addresses at the times of the child abductions.

Hunt, renowned for his impeccable 'contacts' quoted an unnamed former police officer involved with the von Einem report who claimed the report was "significant" because it was compiled before Mr B implicated von Einem in the child abductions during a trial into two Family Murders.

According to Hunt's source the 1989 report, "Examined in detail various areas including von Einem's likeness to the identikit images of suspects, the fact that none of the children were struggling when last seen with the suspect and von Einem's expertise in drugging people."

"The report examined how the children could be taken without putting up a fight or alerting someone to their plight. It pointed out there was a significant amount of evidence already available at that point showed von Einem was skilled at delivering a therapeutic dose of a sedative in order to gain control of a person."

According to the former police officer, the report speculated that if von Einem was involved in the child abductions, "It would have been a simple matter for him to slip sedative drugs into drinks purchased for the children and highlighted that the last sighting of the Beaumont children was at a deli buying soft drinks with money from an unknown source."

"Von Einem's method of operation when seducing his victim was to offer them a drink laced with an undetectable sedative. Once that was achieved he had control over them. They would put up little resistance."

"It was hypothesised in the report that this was a strong explanation for why there were no reports of children struggling at Glenelg or Adelaide Oval. It was quite the contrary, they were seen to be co-operating with the unknown male they were last seen with."

Nigel Hunt's informer said the report also revealed detectives had established von Einem lived at Thebarton at the time of the Adelaide Oval abductions. Von Einem was in fact a resident of Anderson Street, Thebarton in the early 1970s, which is near the last sighting of the mystery man and the abducted girls. The von Einem home was demolished in the mid 1970s when the SA Brewing Company purchased the entire street.

The two senior investigators that led to von Einem's arrest, Detective Robert O'Brien and Detective Trevor Kipling, were adamant that the Family Murders were committed by the same person/s, but Kipling took the killing scenario one step further.

In his book on the Family Murders, *Young Blood*, O'Brien details a conversation he had with Kipling.

O'Brien: The murders were all so similar but after we found out about von Einem, Trevor followed up with a statement which stunned me.

Kipling: You know, I think that he has done the lot.

O'Brien: Yes I know that.

Kipling: Yes, but von Einem has done the Beaumonts, and Ratcliffe and Gordon as well.

O'Brien: Come on . . . bullshit. How can that be? We're looking at boys being murdered— the others were girls.

Kipling: There was a young muscular man seen at Glenelg with the Beaumonts—he had blond hair. Von Einem has been white haired since he was eighteen and he would have been twenty when the Beaumonts went missing. Also, a man was seen with some kids on the banks of the River Torrens when Ratcliffe and Gordon went missing. Why couldn't the same person be responsible?

O'Brien didn't believe Kipling at first. He asked himself, "Why would a person move from picking up girls and murdering them to picking up and killing boys? Intuitively, it didn't make sense".

However, as he reflected on this theory, he thought that it could just be possible. "The youngest of the Beaumont children was a boy. Also, von Einem could have been testing his sexuality at twenty years of age; maybe there was interest in girls, but if the theory was true, more likely the children were just young people who he could abuse—the sex didn't really matter, von Einem was just interested in playing around with bodies".

The saga of the Von Einem 'lookalike' was finally put to rest when a report from an 'expert witness' found no evidence to link the two men.

During February 2009 the Seven Network television programme, *Sunday Night* headed by journalist Ross Coulthart contacted an expert in the field of forensic facial mapping, Kenneth Linge of the UK.

Linge was given two images to examine. One was of Bevan von Einem and the other was the man (male 2) watching a police search at Glenelg only days after the abduction of the children.

After examining both images at length on a high-resolution monitor using software with a considerable magnification capability and a full range of image optimisation tools, Linge concluded that, "When carrying out morphological comparisons I noted that although there are many apparent similarities, close examination revealed apparent differences, as follows."

1. Face shape — There is a slight difference in the slope of the jaw-line from the chin to the ear.

2. Nose — The pronasale and alae are apparently different in shape.

3. The ear shows distinct differences in the shape of the helix, the anti-helix and the lobe, the general shape of the ear is very different in that on male 2; it is more rounded and proportionally larger. Many people believe that the ear is the most unique feature of the human face.

"Despite the apparent facial similarity between the two people, some important differences were noted. Therefore in my opinion these images lend no support to the contention that Bevan von Einem is male 2."

The findings were clear; Bevan Spencer von Einem was not the man in the photo.

Brown, Percy, O'Neil & Co.

Twenty-five years after the disappearance of Joanne Ratcliffe and Kirste Gordon, a former resident of South Australia came forward and claimed to have witnessed the abduction.

Sue Laurie contacted a popular talkback Adelaide radio station FiveAA and revealed to the presenter that as a fourteen-year-old she had observed a young girl fighting with a man who was carrying a little girl near Adelaide Oval on the afternoon of the 1973 abductions. At the time she believed the incident she had witnessed was just a child having an altercation with her grandfather.

Ms Laurie began to "put things together" in 1978 when she contacted SAPOL and gave them a statement on what she saw. She had been constantly disturbed by her recollections of that fateful day.

"I kept on and on at my husband about my memories . . . My husband said 'go and do something about it'".

Ms Laurie later revealed in an interview with the *Sunday Mail* how she and her father had just walked out of the Adelaide Zoo, "We were about midway between Popeye and the University Bridge. I looked across the river and saw a very young girl being carried by a man who I thought was her grandfather. He had a hat and a checked jacket on. She was crying and the older girl, I think she was a few years younger than me, was running after him. She was thumping him and punching into him and crying out at him."

Ms Laurie was certain of the timing of the incident as she recalled hearing the oval siren sounding and her father telling her that the siren marked the start of the game's final quarter. "Dad remarked on the game, but I don't think he saw what I was watching on the other side of the river. I believe on the day of the abduction the police were looking in an opposite direction to where we were walking. The only other thing I need to say is the parents of Joanne should take heart—that little girl did everything she could to protect her little friend".

Ms Laurie decided to come forward with her story after she was horrified when she saw television footage of an old man featured on a news bulletin. Ms Laurie was certain that the abductor she saw back in 1973 was the same man facing charges in a Queensland court. The next day she was desperate to talk to someone about him. She phoned a friend back in Adelaide and let her emotions pour out. She screamed into the phone, "My God! It's him".

The image that haunted Ms Laurie was that of Queenslander Arthur Brown, who was featured on television as well as on the front pages of newspapers around Australia. Brown's facial features were eerily similar to the image of the abductor released soon after Joanne and Kirste went missing. Brown had a thin, gaunt face with hollow cheeks; his deep-set eyes were large with dark rings under them. The identikit back in 1973, which initially looked too gruesome to be real, suddenly had a speculative match.

The publicity surrounding Brown, at one time a school maintenance man, was to do with him being a suspect in the brutal murders in August, 1970 of seven-year-old Judith and five-year-old Susan MacKay, in Townsville, Queensland. The two girls were abducted while on their way to school. They had been raped, stabbed and suffocated. Their dresses were found neatly folded, inside out, beside their school bags, shoes and socks.

Brown's name was brought to the attention of Queensland Police after a woman broke her thirty-year silence and accused Brown of having molested five children related to his first wife. The telling fact was that the alleged offences occurred near the location where the MacKay sisters' bodies were found. Brown was granted bail on forty-five offences against six girls aged between three and ten, during the years from 1970 until 1977. The charges included rape, sodomy, and deprivation of liberty. However, the most intriguing charge was that Brown had been accused of administering a drug.

The ability to administer a drug to victims was perhaps a vital clue in how perpetrators gained control over their victims so easily and rapidly.

Arthur Stanley Brown has at various times been linked with the Adelaide Oval abductions without any hard evidence other than he was a deviant man and under suspicion of heinous crimes against children. However, an eerie coincidence shows that Joanne Ratcliffe and Kirste Gordon disappeared within hours of the third anniversary of the MacKay sisters' abduction.

Brown, who died in 2002, was a wiry but physically strong man who had a number of obsessive behaviours. He was fanatically neat; everything in his life had to be in order. He stood out in his work environment, wearing immaculately pressed clothes while he worked as a carpenter for the Queensland Public Works Department.

South Australian Police have at times worked with their Queensland counterparts to try and establish possible links between the murders of the MacKay schoolgirls and the abduction of the three Beaumont children, as well as the Ratcliffe/Gordon abductions. Canberra Bureau of Crime Intelligence has also been involved. Heading the initial SAPOL Task Force was Superintendent Paul Schramm.

Schramm and his team eventually gathered information that suggested Brown regularly travelled interstate, but no detailed knowledge or exact dates or destinations ever came to light. Police have also speculated that any records of Brown's working records etc. may have been destroyed by Brown himself, who had unsupervised access to numerous government buildings.

There is no conclusive evidence that Brown had ever visited Adelaide, however a relative of his recalled having a conversation with him that may link him to not only Adelaide, but to Adelaide Oval itself. In a passing conversation the relative remembered Brown remarking that he had visited the Adelaide Festival Theatre. The theatre, which was only completed in June 1973, overlooks Adelaide Oval, which sits less than two hundred metres away.

James O'Neill

James Ryan O'Neill was born in 1947 under the name of Leigh Anthony Bridgart. He began his working life in the real-estate industry in his hometown of Melbourne before becoming a gun dealer who was known to have associated with members of Melbourne's criminal underworld.

During the mid to late 1960s, O'Neill immersed himself in the Coober Pedy opal fields, which at the time, could be politely tagged as a 'dodgy' place to do business. Amongst the many honest, hardworking locals were men of dubious reputation. To travel to the South Australian outback town from his home in Melbourne, O'Neill was required to make frequent trips through Adelaide.

In 1971, O'Neill was charged with numerous offences including child abduction and sexual assault on four boys in Victoria. O'Neill was granted bail but anticipating a lengthy jail sentence, he fled interstate. It has been documented that he eventually settled in the north of Western Australia. The lowlight of his time 'out west' was when he was seriously injured from a mysterious incident which ended with him having a bullet lodged in his skull. Later, while working at a cattle station, O'Neill was given his marching orders when the station manager caught the deviant with his pants around his ankles. He was exchanging food he had stolen for sex with young Aboriginal women.

O'Neill had outworn his welcome and headed down south; this time settling in Tasmania.

In February 1975, nine-year-old Ricky John Smith was abducted near his home in Taranna on the Tasman Peninsula while walking to the local shops on an errand for his parents. O'Neill spotted Smith while he was driving to the hospital to see his wife and their newborn baby. O'Neill brazenly abducted and murdered the boy.

With utter contempt, he, along with many locals, helped in the search for the missing boy. Five more children were abducted in the following two weeks in separate incidents around Hobart, but all thankfully managed to escape their attacker. However tragedy followed when nine-year-old Bruce Wilson's body was found after being abducted in the Risdon Vale area in May 1975.

It is unsure why O'Neill became a suspect, but after intense police interrogation, he cracked and led police to the body of Ricky Smith. Even though he was arrested for both of the child murders he only faced a trial for the murder of Smith. O'Neill pleaded guilty on the grounds of insanity; he said it was due to his head injuries from being shot and claimed that police had held a gun to his head to get his confession.

After deliberating for three hours, the jury found O'Neill guilty and he was jailed for life.

O'Neill was an insignificant prisoner, quietly serving his time until freelance journalist Janine Widgery came up with an idea for a documentary. She approached a retired Victorian detective, Gordon Davie, with a proposal to make a documentary on James O'Neill. Davie was not interested in taking part until he read a news report that stated O'Neill had been transferred in 1991 to the low security Hayes Prison Farm and was being allowed to go fishing along the Derwent River unsupervised.

Davie's interest heightened when he read that O'Neill had apparently no criminal record prior to his conviction for murder. Davie couldn't fathom how O'Neill could become a serial killer so late in life. Davie was curious and wrote to O'Neill asking for permission to interview him.

Davie got his wish. O'Neill was adamant that he had never committed any previous crimes other than the murders and abductions he had been charged with. Davie was not convinced with O'Neill's cagey answers and contacted Widgery, telling her he didn't believe a word O'Neill had spoken to him. So began an extraordinary relationship between O'Neill and Davie over four years, in which hundreds of hours of conversations were recorded.

Davie was stunned by O'Neill's persona. "He is one of the most likeable men you would ever meet. On the first day of filming there were six or seven out there and at end of the day I said, 'What do you think of him?' They all said, 'You've made a mistake, this bloke couldn't have done anything wrong'."

Behind the cordial manner of the former detective was a disciplined cop taking in every word from his target. Davie could see patterns emerging from the interviews. O'Neill was not consistent when talking about the times he had visited various locations which were connected to unsolved child murders. According to Davie, O'Neill was hiding many dark secrets.

Davie had information that allegedly placed O'Neill in Adelaide on 26 January 1966. It was even alleged that O'Neill told people he was responsible for the disappearance of the Beaumont children.

Davie asked the child killer the obvious question. "Did you abduct the Beaumont children?"

With no emotion whatsoever, O'Neill replied, "Look, on legal advice I am not going to say where I was or when I was there".

South Australian police have subsequently interviewed O'Neill and discounted him as a suspect in any of the South Australian abductions.

Gordon Davie has a different point of view. "O'Neill didn't deny it (the Beaumonts). That was a very strong point. But he doesn't deny a lot of things he has done".

"He knows a hell of a lot about the Beaumonts. I've never said he was responsible for it, but he'd have to be on the very very short list."

Davie believed it was clear from the Tasmanian murders that O'Neill was an expert at hiding bodies. Davie has even speculated that the Beaumont children may have been thrown down a mineshaft at Coober Pedy after they were abducted.

Davie: "He spoke quite freely when the cameras were rolling. A couple of times he just stopped. One of those was talking about Coober Pedy, and he was telling me that strange things happen."

Davie: "I said, 'What sort of strange things?' and he said, 'Well, people just disappeared off the face of the earth. It happened while I was there'."

O'Neill had told the retired detective that he had travelled from Melbourne to Coober Pedy 15 times.

Davie: "I've also heard from several sources that he had boasted he was responsible for the deaths of the Beaumont children."

Percy

In April 2007, arguably Australia's most revered crime reporter, John Silvester of *The Age*, wrote an intriguing article on Derek Ernest Percy.

The article began in the year of 1969 when Percy (a Navy sailor) was in custody only hours after being apprehended for the abduction and murder of Yvonne Elizabeth Tuohy (12).

Victorian detectives decided to send a former school friend of Percy to his cell to gain more information about his past crimes. The former friend was also a young police constable with only six months experience under his belt.

Senior detectives believed that the Tuohy murder could not have been Percy's first. Back in 1969 Police authorities across Australian were becoming desperate to solve a series of unsolved murders and abductions of children.

1965 — Two young girls, Christine Sharrock and Marianne Schmidt were murdered on Sydney's Wanda Beach.
1966 — The Beaumont children disappeared.
1966 — Allen Redston, (6) — murdered in Canberra.
1968 — Simon Brook, (3) — murdered in Sydney.
1968 — Linda Stilwell, (7) — abducted from St Kilda, Melbourne.

Forty years after the event the young policeman involved revealed to Sylvester the moment he walked into the police cell of his former school friend who was now facing charges of a brutal murder of a child.

Policeman: "He had been sobbing and was very distraught. He said, 'Looks like I've f---ed up this time'. I said, 'It certainly looks like it, Derek'."

Policeman: "Derek put his head in his hands for a while, then he looked up at me again and he had tears in his eyes and panic written all over his face. He also looked at me with a plea for help."

Policeman: "Were there any others, mate?"

"Derek put his head in his hands and began to sob again. He said, 'I can not remember'."

"Well look Derek, I'll ask you about some of the ones that I know about. You don't have to say anything. If you remember I will jot it down and it could be used in court."

The young policeman tried to entice information about Linda Stilwell's disappearance, but Percy said his memory was blank but did admit, "Yes, I drove through St Kilda that day. I had been at Cerberus [Navy base] in the afternoon and was driving along the esplanade on the way to the White Ensign Club for some drinks."

When Percy was asked if he had murdered her, he said, "Possibly, I don't remember a thing about it."

The young police officer kept pressing Percy. When questioned on the murder of Simon Brook, Percy startlingly admitted that he was in Sydney at the time. Percy claimed he had driven his brother to work, turning off at the railway cutting where the body was found.

> Policeman: "So you drove past the same spot in Sydney on the day Simon Brook was killed."
>
> Percy: "Yes".
>
> Policeman: "Do you remember if you killed him?"
>
> Percy: "I wish I could. I might have. I just don't remember."
>
> Policeman: "What do you know about the Beaumont children in South Australia?"
>
> Percy: "I was in Adelaide at the time."
>
> Policeman: "You were what? You remember being in Adelaide when they went missing?"
>
> Percy: "Yes."
>
> Policeman: "Whereabouts were you when they disappeared?"
>
> Percy: "Near the beach. But nothing else."

The Victorian detective's plan of bringing in Percy's former school mate was working remarkably well. Percy obviously trusted the young officer, but in an instant the rapport between them collapsed.

As the two were in deep conversation a prison guard barged into the cell and told the junior constable he had no business being in the cell.

Sylvester: "The young copper said he was on homicide squad business, but when he turned back to Percy the spell was broken. The killer knew his former schoolmate was no longer a friend, but trying to find the secrets of his dark past."

Sylvester: "Was Percy in Adelaide? He told police he had been there on holiday but couldn't remember when. His brother confirmed they had been there. The mother of one of Percy's friends told police: 'I can also recall that Derek travelled to Adelaide on holidays by plane on one occasion'."

"Asked by detectives in 2005 if he was in Adelaide when the Beaumonts went missing he answered, 'I don't know'."

When Sylvester contacted the South Australian Major Crime, Detective Sergeant Brian Swan revealed that Percy remained "a person of interest in the disappearance of the Beaumont children".

16
Satin Man

In 2005, Author, Alan Whiticker and his researcher, Stuart Mullins published the first complete book on the Beaumont disappearance, *Searching for the Beaumont Children*, (John Wiley) to mark the 40th anniversary of the crime.

The book accomplished more than the authors thought possible. Apart from achieving respectable sales success, feedback from readers from across Australia started to flow back to them with fresh new angles for investigation.

One informant would prove to be significant.

In June 2006, Whiticker received a phone call from a woman in Queensland. Amanda claimed that she had been married to a man who was a teenager in Glenelg when the Beaumont children were abducted. The woman went on to reveal that her ex-husband had told her that his father was involved with the children's disappearance!

Whiticker had heard similar allegations many times before

and had a standard reply he often used: "I am not an investigator … I am just a writer." However on this occasion Whiticker listened intently and asked for further information.

"What makes you say that?"

"Because my ex-father-in-law's house was close to where the children were last seen playing and within walking distance of Wenzel's cakes."

"And one more thing, my ex-husband [Warwick] knows where his father buried the children."

In 1966 Warwick's father, Hank, would have been 48-years-old.

Whiticker's Queensland based researcher, Stuart Mullins, interviewed Amanda who did not hold back in her depiction of her ex-husbands father, Hank.

"Warwick's father was a deviant. He was extremely wealthy — and he indulged in a lot of fetishes."

The 'fetish' which was well known amongst family members was Hank's love of satin.

"Warwick's father could not control himself around satin, because he was sexually aroused when he wore satin pyjamas or any other satin clothing".

The satin fetish was hardly a crime but what Amanda revealed next was possibly the first plausible explanation to the mystery of the Beaumont children's 'one pound note'.

"The other thing about your book that really stood out for me was the one pound note. I did not now the children bought lunch with a one-pound note. That rang alarm bells for me. At the time it was an enormous amount of money."

"From a young age Warwick's father would give him and his

friends a pound note to go out on a Saturday afternoon and play at the sideshows so that he could have the house to himself while his wife was out playing tennis … That's when he would dress up in his satin clothes and entertain himself."

Stuart Mullins eventually met with Warwick in October 2007. Warwick had struggled for years with depression, and had constant battles with drug and alcohol abuse but was 'clean' and lucid at the time of the interview.

Mullins: "Do you remember the day the kids went missing, the Beaumont kids on Australia Day, 1966?"

Warwick explained that on that particular afternoon he had just finished work at the local bowling alley.

"When I got home Mum was at the tennis. Dad's car was parked in the driveway." Warwick went on to describe how he and some friends were 'smoking ciggies' in a cubby house in the backyard, when he saw three children come through the back gate.

He said they looked lost. The three children went inside the house, but Warwick didn't see them come out. He did, however, see Hank load up the boot of the car with four large bags about an hour later.

Hank drove away, but Warwick did not see the children get into the car.

During the interview Warwick told Mullins where he believed the Beaumont children were buried, "They're in the sandpit."

The 'sandpit' was a reference to the business property owned by his father.

The revealing interview with Warwick has to be put into context. Warwick has also claimed that his father had sexually abused him as a child for numerous years. Were his revelations a bitter 'pay back' for his father's alleged appalling crimes against him? Was it possible that Warwick's prolonged bouts of drug and alcohol abuse were a factor in his recollections?

When Hank died he left a fortune to his family. Were Warwick's allegations related to an inheritance battle?

Whiticker and Mullins published their investigations of Hank in July 2013. *The Satin Man* book (New Holland) had an immediate impact.

Adelaide's *Today Tonight* current affairs programme featured the new information regarding Hank, which brought forward a most extraordinary new clue to the case.

While *Satin Man* kept the identity of Hank a secret, Channel Seven revealed that the 'Satin Man' was none other than Harry Phipps, the former owner of the successful Castalloy business at Plympton who died in 2003.

The programme triggered the memories of two brothers who watched the show. They recalled that in late January 1966, as teenagers, they were asked by Phipps to dig a hole at the rear of his factory plant.

According to the brothers, the hole was the size of a large grave. The digging of the large hole was not easy in the summer heat but they were paid handsomely by the millionaire industrialist. At the time the brothers didn't think anything of it, although they occasionally recounted the story about a man who drove a Pontiac Parisienne who had watched them dig that hole.

After viewing the *Today Tonight* story, the brothers questioned themselves. Had they been employed as grave diggers for the Beaumont children!

They immediately contacted S.A. Police, *Today Tonight* and authors, Whiticker and Mullins.

Bill Hayes, a private investigator and former SAPOL detective, who had helped the authors of Satin Man, was interviewed by *Today Tonight* regarding the brothers' memories.

Hayes: "They're incredibly good, credible intelligent witnesses. They can't be criticized for not having clear recollections of this event, it was 47 years ago; I'm surprised they'd remembered as much as they had".

After the television programme was aired, S.A. Major Crime detectives declared that Harry Phipps was not a suspect in the case and that the allegations implicating him had been thoroughly investigated and discounted back in 2007 when Whiticker and Mullins contacted them with their research on the deceased businessman.

A relative of the Phipps family came forward and contacted *The Advertiser* to defend the deceased man's reputation.

"There is no way these allegations would ever have been published if Harry was still alive. So just because someone is dead and is not here to defend themselves legally, it makes it all right to do this to someone and their family".

When Major Crime officer-in-charge, Detective Superintendent Des Bray was queried about a possible excavation at Phipps' former factory, he replied, "At this time there is no information that would justify the excavation of any property."

However, SAPOL decided to end the mystery of the Castalloy 'sand pit' in January 2014 by using ground-penetrating radar (GPR) borrowed from the Australian Federal Police to search the area.

During that examination the GPR found one small anomaly, however an excavation of a one-square-metre section of the site found no additional evidence of anything having been buried at the site.

Assistant Commissioner Paul Dickson declared the investigation into the site and its former owner were now closed.

"The investigative opportunity related to Castalloy is now complete".

"The longer the time goes it lessens our opportunity to resolve this matter, but we only need one or two pieces of information which will resolve the jigsaw." "Every case can be solved; obviously some cases are more likely to be solved than others ... all we need is that integral bit of information."

In July 2015, I visited Mostyn Matters, the retired S.A. Police officer who was attached to the Beaumont investigation from the very first day. He was adamant that there should be a full and thorough excavation of the factory site.

Even after 50 years Matters is still upset when he talks about the investigation that failed to uncover any suspects or evidence. "It was not to do with a lack of trying. We all worked tirelessly." "Blighty (Detective Ron Blight) took it to heart. He never got over it."

Matters who became life-long friends with Grant and Nancy, believes that the Phipps lead is the most plausible link in the Beaumont mystery that has come to light and can't understand why SAPOL don't want to pursue it further.

"There are too many co-incidences."

"Where Phipps lived — the one pound note."

"It's the best clue in my opinion."

17
What's New?

Investigative journalism in South Australia throughout the late 1990s and 2000s was dominated by the multiple award winning journalist Nigel Hunt of *The Advertiser/Sunday Mail* and Graham Archer of Adelaide's *Today Tonight*; a current affairs show on the Seven Network.

Hunt joined *The News* in 1982 and spent 10 years as a police reporter before joining *The Advertiser* in 1992 when *The News* was finally closed down. Hunt's solid foundation at the coalface of crime reporting enabled him to nurture an amazing number of contacts which fuelled many of his articles.

Archer on the other hand started out as a school teacher before becoming a television news reporter. Often referred to as a 'maverick', Archer has become a 'lone wolf' in his constant battle against injustice within South Australia. Not afraid to make enemies with his exposes Archer has become legendary; stirring the pot without fear or favour.

However a new kid on the block began to make a name for himself in Adelaide's journalistic circles in 2012. Bryan Littley of News Corp. wrote a series of articles from 2012-2015 that would again put the mystery of the missing children of Adelaide back in the headlines.

In 2012 Littley highlighted the Adelaide Oval abduction case with information gained from a group of mysterious 'private investigators'. The investigators had spent almost three years searching for clues to the case after they had obtained confidential documents from State Archive files in connection with the 'Mullighan Inquiry' (Commission of Inquiry into Children in State Care).

Their search took them to a 'ghost town' known as Yatina; situated between the Mid North towns of Jamestown and Ororoo. The investigators had in their possession a hand drawn map with intricate details of the possible whereabouts of the remains of Joanne Ratcliffe and Kirste Gordon.

The investigators spent weeks searching the surrounds of a Yatina farmhouse but no sign of the children's bodies were found, however some key 'clues' were uncovered. The items of interest included an Akubra type hat, which they speculated matched the one worn by the suspected abductor, a medical book and numerous newspaper clippings detailing the Adelaide Oval abductions.

The most intriguing find was found submerged in murky water, in a tunnel under a dam. Two large metal drums were discovered that contained a honeycomb-like substance. The investigators took the material to an unknown source for 'testing' where it was claimed to be positive for blood.

When a sample of the substance was given a presumptive test by S.A. Police Forensic Services, it was found to have only a "weak to very weak" trace of blood. After a more thorough test for haemoglobins was conducted, SAPOL came out and declared the substance was "Insignificant to the case."

The author of the 'confidential documents' was hardly a reliable source. Mark Marshall, a convicted paedophile wrote the information while serving time in Yatala Prison for numerous offences against children. Police had known of Marshall's essays and dismissed them outright as a, "Fabrication from the writer's imagination."

Yatina

While S.A. Police had publicly poured cold water on the validity of Marshall's documents, something in the private investigators findings must have rung true. So much so, that in September 2014 Major Crime Detectives along with STAR Group personnel searched various sites in Yatina looking for clues into the Ratcliffe and Gordon case.

It was now clear that there was a known connection between the Yatina district and a 'person of interest' in the abduction case.

STAR Group officers and forensic investigators concentrated their efforts on two wells at various locations but after a number of days excavating, Detective Inspector Greg Hutchins said that nothing of importance had been found.

Hutchins said the searches were the result of a call to Crime Stoppers and the culmination of information police had gathered over time. Importantly he confirmed that, "The previous occupant of the Yatina property is one of a number of people who have been linked to the girls' disappearance over the years, but to date police have been unable to substantiate his involvement."

"The man has previously been interviewed by detectives, but died in 1999."

"To date no evidence has been found at the well site, so there's a possibility the man who owned the property years ago may not be responsible for the girls' disappearance."

"This search is about finalising one line of inquiry."

Underground Bunker

In March 2015, Littley published a sensational story regarding yet another 'fresh lead' in the Ratcliffe/Gordon abduction case. He wrote that there was now "Proof that puts a key suspect at the ground [Adelaide Oval] on the day of the crime which links him to an abandoned Prospect home with an underground bunker."

The suspect in question was a known paedophile, Stanley Arthur Hart, whose Yatina property was searched by Major Crime in 2013/14. Coincidently he was also a close relative of Mark Marshall.

Hart's family had come forward and claimed that Stanley Hart "almost certainly" would have been at Adelaide Oval on August 25, 1973, when Ratcliffe and Gordon were abducted. They said that even though Hart did not attend the Adelaide Oval match between North and Norwood with them, Hart "Rarely missed a Roosters footy match."

They also stated that Hart lived in a Prospect property and

had "unrestricted and unmonitored access" to the abandoned home during the years 1973-74.

What made this Prospect property so newsworthy was when *The Advertiser* published a photograph of Hart in the backyard. He posed for the camera cradling a rifle, standing in front of a large underground bunker, which was described in the article as an "air-raid shelter". It apparently was large enough to fit at least four adults and was demolished some time before 1975.

Littley also published in his article a statement made by Marshall to the Mullighan Inquiry back in 2007, "Poppa Stan [Hart] had taken a hat and a coat from 'grandad's house' to wear at the footy that day."

The theory put forward by the 'private investigators' was that they believed the abductor could have taken Ratcliffe and Gordon out of the parklands, that surrounded the Adelaide Oval on a 'Red Hen' train from the North Adelaide train station. This, they believed fitted in with the last reported sighting of the girls, at around 5 p.m. with their abductor, near Port Road; a short distance from the North Adelaide station.

The Advertiser also passed on to SAPOL a number of other leads from the private investigators and members of the public.

- A known child abuser revealed a decade after their disappearance, that he saw Joanne and Kirste with their abductor;
- The same man was an avid North Adelaide Football Club fan and lived close to Prospect Oval and had the shell of a car buried in his backyard;
- An anonymous caller to *The Advertiser*, using voice

distortion, said a Prospect address is a place of interest in the Adelaide Oval case and that US Air force fuel barrels are reportedly buried at a location in Adelaide's north and contain evidence in the case.
- A number of items including a butcher's apron and pants reportedly belonging to Hart and removed from the Yatina property by a third party before police searches commenced was handed to police.

Mr X
June 2015

Only three months after his expose regarding the Adelaide Oval abductions, Littley produced an explosive article regarding a possible suspect in the Beaumont case.

The opening paragraph read:

"Vigilante paedophile hunters are tracking the movements of a former Adelaide businessman and convicted paedophile in South-East Asia in a bid to solve a child abduction case there."

According to the article, the suspect, Mr X, who reportedly lives in South-East Asia, is aged in his mid seventies and was described as "a flamboyant man about town". He was being pursued by a former Adelaide business associate and two other men; a "bounty hunter" who claimed to be an ex-American intelligence agent and a "senior police officer".

Littley claimed Mr X was assisting the vigilantes in their investigation of the disappearance of two children, aged four and six, in the Asian city where he now lives.

Apparently Mr X once confided to his former business partner that, "I've done some very bad things", before cashing in millions of dollars of business interests and fleeing the country.

This story then becomes extraordinary.

The claims against Mr X were backed up by Maxwell McIntyre a man S.A. Police had previously investigated regarding the alleged involvement in the Beaumont children's abduction!

Mr McIntyre, a former sailor and union powerbroker told Littley that "Mr X, a convicted paedophile, was involved in the abduction and likely had help."

His claims were documented in a number of sworn statements given to SAPOL.

SAPOL naturally refused to confirm if they had investigated Mr X but Littley claimed "It is known the Mr X moved to South-East Asia shortly after he was named in material investigated by the S.A. Major Crime Unit."

McIntyre (85) was adamant that Mr X was involved in the Beaumont abduction. "He has (done it) ... deeply involved."

"He is one of the most evil pieces of work that ever drew breath."

McIntyre revealed he had information that placed Mr X at the Glenelg Beach, the day the Beaumont children disappeared.

Bodies in a car

McIntyre was cleared by SAPOL of any involvement in the Beaumont case back in 2007, after police followed up an allegation that was broadcast on national television.

Three of his children appeared (disguised) on '*Crime Investigation Australia*'. One claimed they saw three children's bodies in the back of McIntyre's car at the time of the Beaumonts disappearance.

The adult children of McIntyre alleged their father had abused them and that their father was part of a paedophile ring which operated in and around Adelaide in the 1960s. During the interview they also alleged that their "Father, a family friend, and others, were involved in the disappearance of the Beaumont children".

When the children were asked why they hadn't come forward sooner. One of the siblings responded: "I think you have to grow up in a family and have that much trauma and abuse. You can't live with these things every day and I guess there is a point where you put it in a box and I suppose I had to survive psychologically."

"It was difficult as a child; I could never do anything about my position. Who was I going to tell — I always felt I was putting other people at risk."

Another family member added: "All the pieces started to come together — it was quite phenomenal really. My sister in particular — she's been incredible, her memory is fantastic and I understand that when you have something so traumatic happen to you, you remember it with such clarity it's incredible, way back 30 years ago I can remember what my father was wearing when he abused me."

Mr McIntyre was asked if he believed the claims made by his children regarding the children's bodies in the back of his car.

"(But) I didn't even own the car and it never happened …. When I was there."

"I believe (Mr X) is up to his eyeballs in this."

Mr McIntyre said if the full claims were to be believed, the bodies of the children allegedly taken to his former home were burned in the incinerator of his backyard.

He added that his children, who made the claims, "know something".

Mr McIntyre's daughter, Ruth Collins came forward in 2015 and suggested there were up to 10 people at the scene that may have information about the abduction and murder of the Beaumont children.

Collins: "All I've ever done is tell authorities — try to tell the authorities — what I saw and what I heard."

"I was 10½ at the time but I was mature. I collected up all the information that I didn't understand and waited to find out what was going on."

"I wish I'd never remembered. My life would be easier."

Vietnam Vet spoke to 'Jane'

Littley published a story in *The Advertiser* on August 29, 2015 regarding another 'potential witness' who believed he had not only spoken to Jane Beaumont but also to a young man that could possibly be the abductor of the Beaumont children.

The witness gave a statement to police after seeing a missing person's poster in a police station in May 2015. The man believed he had spoken to Jane, 9, just minutes before she and her siblings were taken from Glenelg in a vehicle he described as "distinctive".

The potential witness, who was 20 at the time, said he was eating lunch near Wenzels Bakery when he spoke to a girl he believes was Jane.

"A lad about my age had come up from the beach and used the shower," his statement to police says.

"He had three children with him. A girl about 11, a girl about 6, and a boy about 4. The eldest girl was quite chatty and sat on the bench I was on.

"She looked at my lunch. I asked her was she hungry and she said no (the lad) had given them a pound and they had lunch from the bakery."

"I spoke to the lad, asking him if he had had his National Service call up. He answered no, he hadn't, I had. End of conversation."

The young man in question was described as being of medium height and build with sandy coloured hair and had an Australian accent. He was wearing distinctive, European-style bathers.

The witness said all four then got into a car and left, travelling north. *The Advertiser* has chosen not to publish the detailed description of the distinctive vehicle.

He said he had never come forward because he was not aware what he had seen that could be connected to the case.

"Anything I had ever read about the Beaumont children, it was always linked to the Bay Sheffield running race and Colley Reserve," he said.

"I've never been to that race and I don't know the reserve. I never thought anything of it. Nothing fitted with what I saw and a crime. There just didn't seem to be anything wrong."

The witness who had been conscripted for the Vietnam War effort, was flown to Puckapunyal, Victoria, a week after the children went missing

"We had no television and no SA papers," he said. "I was away for two years — and I didn't come back in very good shape."

(The Bay Sheffield footrace has been held at Colley Reserve,

Glenelg every year since 1887 on Proclamation Day, the day South Australians celebrates its birthday — December 28th. However in the years 1966-1969 the race was held at Wigley Reserve due to construction work being carried out between the Town Hall and Colley Reserve.)

18
Who Could Do Such a Thing?

A crime such as the abduction of the Beaumont children could only have been carried out by a minute percentage of the Australian population. The thought processes and actions of such a deviant are so far removed from society's norms and agreed behaviour code that it is incomprehensible for most of us to fathom how a fellow human could commit such an atrocity.

Most of us, thankfully, never have to deal with their sordid fantasies or their stomach-churning actions. However, there are specialists whose job it is to study and converse with them (while in custody) and finally, build a profile on how they act, both before and after their crimes.

In the mid-1970s the FBI established a branch in its operations that dealt exclusively with profiling child sex offenders. To understand what could possibly motivate a crime such as the Beaumont abductions, we can delve into the work of two of the world's most credentialed experts in this field.

As an FBI agent, John Douglas was one of the world's first criminal profilers. Douglas believes child molesters are like any other criminal; they exhibit specific behaviours both before and after committing their crimes. These 'fingerprints' can help reveal their identity. Fellow FBI agent, Ken Lanning, who is a leading specialist on the research into crimes against children, has defined various types of child molesters:

True paedophiles: People who prefer sex with children and have them as the subjects of their fantasies.

Preferential child molesters: Whose primary sexual drives and fantasies are directed at adults, but who will have sex with a child to fulfill some other need. They often feel too inadequate to approach the true object of their desires, using a child as a substitute. The child is more a victim of opportunity than a preferential victim.

Situational molesters: Just as not all paedophiles are molesters, not all molesters are paedophiles. A variety of motivations may drive the so-called 'situational molester'. Some molesters may act out their aggression because they are only capable of expressing themselves against the most vulnerable of victims. Lanning believes the risk with these individuals is that their behaviour will escalate. "What may begin as an impulsive, isolated event against a child may turn out to be just a trial run if he succeeds without getting caught. Their crimes may grow more violent; grow bolder as their criminal career progresses, attacking more victims and taking more time with them to act out their fantasies more completely".

Sexual predators can also change their targets to suit their current fantasy. An example of this was highlighted by Douglas in his book, *Into the Darkness*. He detailed a case in Rochester, New

York, which involved a killer of women who regularly returned to the dump-sites to spend more time with the bodies of his victims. "Once he was caught, it turned out that his first two victims had not been prostitutes or homeless women, but a young girl and boy".

Douglas explained, "The sexually indiscriminate molester, if asked why they molested a child, might think to themselves, 'why not?' These molesters take that thought a step further. He abuses children because he is bored and the experience seems new, exciting and different to him. These types are labelled 'try-sexuals,' meaning that they'll try anything."

A tri-sexual perpetrator is not so much naturally sexually attracted to children as he is sexually curious with insecurities around adults. Douglas: "He is so withdrawn from society; the danger is that his hostility and anger could build up until he finds an outlet for them. This subject can be very dangerous, then, if his rage explodes, it can often lead to torturing and killing his victim".

The two FBI specialists both agree that the most dangerous preferential child molester is the 'sadistic type'. Like sadistic rapists and killers of adults, they need to cause pain—physical, and or psychological, to be aroused and satisfied sexually.

"A sadistic type of molester will use either trickery or force to gain control of his victims and then torture them in some way for his sexual gratification. Although there seem to be few sadistic molesters, these are the most likely to abduct and murder their victims."

Lanning describes the four phases of abduction by an offender: build up, abduction, post abduction and recovery/release.

"In the build up the subject engages in fantasy that creates some need for sexual activity, although it may not start out child-orientated. He validates and rationalises his fantasy by talking to others who share or encourage it or by looking at pornographic material that fuels it. There could be a precipitating stressor that prompts the subject to act on his fantasies, and then either an opportunity presents itself or the offender plans and creates one. When the subject is ready to carry out the abduction, victim selection becomes the key".

Lanning believes that a predator may choose a complete stranger so that it can't be linked back to him. "It is critical to his odds of not getting caught".

Lanning labels these criminals as 'thought-driven offenders'. They plan a 'mode of operation' (MO) and stick to it. They weigh up the risks and use opportunities to their advantage, selecting a victim who fits a broad profile. This type of offender (who has planned ahead and exercised discipline in victim selection) has a much greater chance of getting away with their crimes.

The 'fantasy-driven' abductor, on the other hand, is more concerned with his ritual. He might script the abduction with a very specific type of victim in mind and then not be flexible enough to modify or deviate from his plan even if it increases his risks. This compulsiveness, driven by such specific needs, makes it more difficult for him to carry off the abduction successfully.

A landmark report on child abduction/murders was prepared in 2006 by members of the Attorney General's Dept. in Washington USA.

Some of the findings were startling.
- The researchers found that it was common for child abductors to be at the initial 'victim-killer contact site'

for a *legitimate reason*. They either lived in the area or were engaged in some normal activity.
- One of the most intriguing facts is that during an investigation into child abductions, t*he name of the killer* is likely to be in the investigative file *within the first week*!
- Furthermore, the findings show that "It is not uncommon for the police to have actual contact with the killer before he becomes a primary suspect, for example, during the initial neighbourhood canvass."
- The typical victim is near his or her home when last seen prior to the abduction, and that often the *killer is not far away*.
- In 36.5% of the child murders, the killer lived within 500 metres of the initial contact site.

Profile of a child abductor/murderer

The clique profile of a child molester/abductor as being the proverbial 'dirty old man' has in recent years been comprehensively debunked by criminologists world-wide.

According to the Washington AG report, the average age of killers of abducted children is around 27-years-old. In fact 55 percent of child abductor/killers are 25-years-old or younger. "They are predominantly unmarried, and half of them either live alone or with their parents. Half of them are unemployed, and those that are employed work in unskilled or semi-skilled labour occupations."

Other findings revealed that:
- Child killers are generally characterized as being "social marginal's."

- Almost two-thirds of the killers have prior arrests for violent crimes, with slightly more than half of those prior crimes committed against children. The most frequent prior crimes against children are rape and other types of sexual assault. Most of the murderers' prior crimes are similar in the MO to the child abduction murder.
- 76.9% had committed crimes to children prior to the murder/abduction.

'Occam's Razor' is a principle that has been attributed to a 14th century Franciscan friar, William of Ockham, who drew on his minimalistic and frugal lifestyle to produce a philosophy on problem solving.

There are many varied descriptions of his theory but it can be best summarised, "When you have two competing theories that make exactly the same predictions, the simpler one is the better."

Or if you want a layman's version: "The simplest answer is most often correct."

This principle is often used in the field of science and has gained a following among criminologists.

Using this "keep it simple" philosophy let us look at the 'known' facts of the Beaumont case.

Jane, Arnna and Grant Beaumont were seen as they walked hand in hand away from their home in Harding Street, Somerton Park towards Diagonal Road on the morning of January 26, 1966. This is possibly the only undisputed fact in the whole abduction saga. Nancy Beaumont and a neighbour who lived directly opposite witnessed this event.

The time of the children's departure is ambiguous. In every media publication directly after the abduction and right up to this very day the time has been documented at 9.45 a.m., so they could catch the 10 a.m. bus to Glenelg. Even SAPOL clearly states '9.45 a.m.' as the official time in their 'Resume of the investigation'; however Nancy Beaumont in a 1968 interview explicitly states the children left at 8.35 a.m.

And what can we make of the witnesses that came forward?

Recent studies on the validity of witness statements have uncovered the issues police have in dealing with 'eye witness' accounts.

In a Laura Engelhardt article on witness statements she writes; "Rarely do we tell a story or recount events without a purpose. Every act of telling and retelling is tailored to a particular listener; we would not expect someone to listen to every detail of our morning commute, so we edit out extraneous material. The act of telling a story adds another layer of distortion, which in turn affects the underlying memory of the event."

There were three crucial sightings of what was thought to be the Beaumont children; the first was at Colley Reserve, then at Wenzel's Cake Shop; and the final positive sighting was by Patterson the postman.

Were the children at Colley Reserve seen playing and communicating with the 'surfie' man the Beaumont children?

During the investigation, detectives working on the case were baffled by the actions of the man playing with the children. If he was the abductor why did he brazenly walk up to a potential witness and ask them about money being stolen from his belongings? His actions are hardly that of a sophisticated criminal planning an extraordinary crime. On the other hand, why has this man remained silent when his description has been published Australia wide?

The children who purchased one pie, numerous pasties, and two large bottles of soft-drink along with cakes with a one pound note; were they the Beaumont children? Nancy Beaumont gave the children only a sufficient amount of coins so they could buy their lunch and their bus ticket home. Either the Beaumont children were given the one pound note by their abductor or the children were another set of three children altogether.

During the 1960s it was not uncommon for parents to send their children to the shops to buy their lunch. How positive was the identification of these children? Why did police delay releasing this information to the public for 12 months? Did they doubt the validity of this sighting?

The last sighting by the Beaumont's postman turned out to be a bizarre turn of events. Patterson at first told police he saw them in the afternoon between the hours of 1.45 p.m. and 2.55 p.m. The following day he spoke to police and changed the time frame to mid morning.

When questioned a week or so later by former NSW detective, Ray Kelly, Patterson reverted to his original belief that he had seen the children at 2.50 p.m. Patterson knew the Beaumont children by sight and so his evidence is vital in trying to establish the time the Beaumonts disappeared; but which version of events is the truth?

The 'identikit'

Almost every article on the Beaumont mystery for the past 50 years has always been accompanied by a gruesome looking image of a thin faced man.

The authenticity of the identikit image of the man wanted in connection with the Beaumont mystery was irreparably damaged in 2001 when an ABC Radio National program revealed that the artist responsible for sketching the 'thin-face man' was possibly drunk at the time. The interview with the newspaper artist was a revealing insight into the meagre information police had at their disposal to solve the crime.

"Unfortunately at the time I had been drinking heavily in my tea break, and I didn't quite understand at the time until I'd sobered — and it made me sober very quickly I can tell you when I got down there — to discover that the police were relying on that, plus the paper had opened the front page, for the story. Nothing more sobering than that."

"We had two people come forward and try to describe, but unfortunately the police never had any real equipment in terms of an identikit that they could use, so they were using artists — on one of the very few occasions they ever did this — they used artists, and it was very difficult for me because the woman really couldn't describe it, and as soon as you started using association, she started to lose it."

The only specific feature the artist received from the witnesses was that the man had a thin face, "So I just drew a very thin-faced person, thinking this was not going to amount to anything ... So I never really completed the drawing because it wasn't complete enough."

The newspaper artist tried in vain to get more information from the witnesses to work with.

"Do you know what colour his hair was? Was it receding?" 'Oh, I'm not sure.' Does he look like this? We kept sort of drawing and the detective … And more and more people came in, and the television people arrived, and it got out of hand."

"The actual purpose of the woman being there sort of somehow got lost in the circus, and I felt at the time, that because it was such a serious case, it may have been handled better if they'd taken us all away to a place."

In July 2015 I spoke to Mostyn Matters, the police officer who was at the front desk of the Glenelg Police Station when Grant and Nancy Beaumont rushed in to inform him that their children were missing. Matters claimed that he and his colleagues were always sceptical of the 'surfie man' suspect. "It just didn't seem right".

How did the abduction occur?

The most puzzling part of this case is the 'how'. How could three children disappear in the middle of the day in front of with thousands of witnesses?

The most discussed scenario has been where a person or persons somehow enticed the children into a vehicle. Even though 'Stranger Danger' was not yet a widespread mantra parents in the mid 1960s were fully aware of the dangers that faced their children.

Jane was only nine-years-old, but she was mature enough not to enter a vehicle of a stranger. On the other hand, the day was so stifling hot the children would have welcomed the opportunity to get a lift home offered by a person known to them; especially as four-year-old Grant would have been struggling with the heat.

Grant Beaumont Snr. offered a plausible scenario a few months after the abduction. He speculated that perhaps his children were told by the abductor that their father had returned from his business trip and sent this person to pick them up.

Three children entering a vehicle would not have been a noteworthy action on such a day.

But surely when the children realised that they were not heading home there would have been a 'sighting' of struggling children in a car?

And is it possible that when the abductor arrived at his destination there was not one witness?

The 'abducted by vehicle' scenario relies on many speculative assumptions.

We can simplify the abduction by making one straightforward but significant assumption: 'The children decided to walk home from Glenelg beach as they had done only one day before.'

Nancy Beaumont was expecting her children to arrive via a bus, but also knew her children were capable and had previous experience in walking home.

This assumption narrows down the possibilities.

Could the children have been enticed by a person into a property while walking home? Was there a known child sex offender on the route from the Glenelg foreshore to the Beaumonts home?

The Washington researchers detailed an investigation process that enhances the chances of solving an abduction/murder.

The report detailed the four most important crime 'sites'.

1. The 'Initial Contact' site, 2. the 'Victim Last Seen' site; 3. the 'Murder' site and 4. the 'Body Recovery' site.

The Beaumont case unfortunately doesn't have a murder or a body recovery site. However the Initial Contact site and the Victim Last Seen site bring together some interesting facts to ponder.

According to the report the Victim's Last Seen site was within 400 metres of the Initial Contact site in 79.4% of child abduction murder cases. Also, in 40.3% of the murders, the Victim Last Seen site was less than 60 metres from the victim's home. In 36.1%, the Victim Last Seen site was 400 metres from the killer's home.

Another misconception attached to child abduction is that killers keep children alive for long periods of time after the abduction. According to the Washington AG report, missing children were killed within a very short period of time after their abduction. 46.8% were killed within one hour of the abduction, 76.2% within three hours and 88.5% within 24 hours.

The possibility that the Beaumont children were abducted and murdered by a Glenelg resident is a strong one. The simple task of inviting the children into a home for refreshments by the abductor would have looked safe to Jane, especially if that person was a young adult. Perhaps this young adult was Jane's mystery 'boy friend' that was mentioned to Nancy Beaumont by Arnna a week or so before the abduction.

It is quite possible that the precious souls of the three children are buried at a Glenelg property; but where do you start digging?

A speculative thought ... or two

During my research there was an unusual yet highly tenuous coincidence connecting the Beaumonts and the Ratcliffe/Gordon abductions.

Early in the Beaumont search, Brighton businessman, Barry Blackwell, visited the home of Grant and Nancy to offer his support to the grieving parents. Whilst discussing her children, Nancy mentioned that the children loved to play amongst the large painted concrete pipes at the Veale Gardens playground; part of Adelaide's southern CBD parklands.

Veale Gardens was also where Kirste Gordon had been photographed shortly before her disappearance.

So what? You may ask. Many South Australians will know that Veale Gardens has been infamous since the 1960s. Right up to recent years this area of the parklands had been the epicentre for paedophiles in Adelaide to gather and 'trade'.

Commissioner Ted Mullighan, in his report on the sexual abuse of wards of the state, identified Veale Gardens as a known paedophile haunt. He documented cases of children soliciting themselves for sexual favours for as little payment as a Coke and a hamburger.

Could the Beaumonts and Kirste Gordon have been targeted and stalked?

The 'connection' is probably even stretching the boundaries of speculation; nevertheless nothing in these two baffling crimes has ever made any sense; and nothing would surprise me what the devious minds of child murderers are capable of.

The only factor that has linked all of South Australian child abduction/murders is that all the crimes were committed during school holidays.

Could an itinerant worker who had only frequented Adelaide during school holidays be the killer?

During the initial search, Grant Beaumont mentioned how his children enjoyed going to the 'sideshow ally' at Glenelg Beach but he had warned his children not to go there without him. The sideshows were mainly populated at nightfall but could the children

18 Who Could Do Such a Thing?

have met their abductor there?

It was reported that a man matching the description of the '6 ft. surfie' was seen by local residents "lurking" around the sideshows in the days leading up to the abduction.

When you bring into the equation details such as 'itinerant worker' — 'sideshow ally'; people with a historical understanding of child murders in South Australia will recall the tragic death on Saturday 20 December 1958, of Mary Olive Hattam.

The nine-year-old girl was brutally murdered near the South Australian town of Ceduna 768 km from Adelaide. A former boxer, Rupert Maxwell Stuart was working at a nearby traveling funfair when he was arrested for the horrific murder.

On the day of her death, Mary was playing with her brother (10) and another boy on the beach. The boys went off on their own, and between 2 p.m. and 4 p.m. Mary disappeared. Her body was later found in a cave. She had been sexually assaulted and her head had been savagely bashed with a rock.

Stuart, (27) an Arrernte man, was charged with the murder. At first Stuart denied any involvement in the murder, but following a prolonged police interview he confessed to killing the child. But the method of obtaining Stuart's 'confession' — the most vital piece of evidence against him — quickly came under fire.

Stuart alleged police had beaten and choked him, and linguistic experts claimed that a man with Stuart's limited English could not have given the articulate account police swore he gave.

Stuart was found guilty of murder and was given the 'death penalty'. His conviction was the subject of several appeals to higher courts, as well as a Royal Commission; all of which upheld the verdict.

However, the Adelaide newspaper, *The News* led by a youthful Rupert Murdoch campaigned successfully against the death penalty being imposed. Stuart served his time in prison and consistently claimed his innocence right up until his death in 2014.

We will never know for certain if Stuart murdered Mary Hattam in 1958 but *if* Stuart was innocent, could the killer have also been a member of the traveling group of 'carnies'? Did the killer move onto another 'traveling' group and end up in Adelaide in 1966 and 1973?

The 'carnies' image was tainted at a coronial investigation in 2003 into the murder of Stacey Lee Kirk, at the Maitland Show in 1984. Coroner John Abernethy touched on what he called the "brotherhood" within the show circuit.

"On the evidence before me, showmen and show workers are a difficult breed of 'suspects', if I can put it that way. They are clannish and close and they are on the move."

Child abduction/murders are thankfully few and far between. Multiple abduction/murders are extraordinary rare; in fact finding similar abductions to Adelaide's in the western world has been a futile exercise.

Could two separate criminals pull off two extraordinary crimes without either one of them getting caught? What are the odds? The crimes seem to be linked…

In recent years, SAPOL, under the leadership of Superintendent Des Bray (Head of Major Crime), has produced some outstanding results in regards to so called 'cold cases'. Since 2014 these murder investigations are being co-ordinated by a new 'special operations team' after Police Commissioner Gary

Burns allocated an extra 14 officers to Major Crime.

One such case will play out in a South Australian court in late 2015/16. Unfortunately because of strict court orders no details of this crime can be published.

19
Gone But Never Forgotten

Could a crime such as the Beaumont children abduction ever happen in today's 'tech savvy', 'child protection aware' world?

The answer unfortunately is a resounding YES; although the chances of the abductor getting caught are much higher than fifty years ago. Police forensic technology, increased police resources and the 'intrusion' of CCTV cameras into our society have made fighting crime much more efficient.

In March 2015 I attended a World Cup cricket match at the 'revamped' Adelaide Oval. Twenty thousand people enjoyed what turned out to be a wonderful celebration of world sport; Australia v Pakistan.

Sitting in front of me, high up in the grandstand were a husband and wife with two daughters, approximately nine and eleven years of age. During the game I saw the mother hand the girls a fifty dollar note. I was disturbed as I watched the girls skip down the stairs and head behind the grandstand.

It was close to twenty minutes before the happy faces of the girls came up the stairs with a drink and ice cream in hand.

I thought to myself about how many times this scene is played out during a year across Australia, probably in the thousands, more likely in the tens of thousands. Then I thought of the probability of a deviant being part of these sporting events, knowing that child molesters frequent such events to 'get their kicks'.

As protectors of our children, should we be playing this game of 'chance'?

Child abduction murders are rare events, however as a community, it is our responsibility to eliminate, or at least minimise the opportunity for our children to become victims.

According to the Washington AG report, the first step towards child safety is to be aware that children are not immune from abduction just because they are close to home. In fact, well over half of the abductions that led to murder took place in close proximity to the child's home.

"Perhaps the most important single thing we can do as parents to protect our children is to be certain that our children are supervised, even if they are in their own front yard or neighbourhood street."

The term 'stranger danger' has been a useful mantra used across the world in regards to the safety of children. It has educated children that they should "never speak to strangers" and "never get into cars with strangers"

Experts have now taken the warnings one step higher and are demanding that children be educated to *"never even approach a car, whether the occupant of the car is a stranger or not, no matter what they tell or ask them."*

Grant and Nancy

My aspiration for this book was to record an accurate history of this crime and the enormous impact it had on Australians at the time. The shock, sadness and the inevitable fear Australians felt, faded over time, but for Grant and Nancy it has been fifty years of misery. Somehow, with amazing inner fortitude they have managed to cope and live through one of the most tragic personal crisis a human could ever endure.

Grant and Nancy Beaumont separated during the 1980s; the stress of the abduction finally tore them apart.

Grant turned ninety in August 2015; Nancy had her eighty-eighth birthday in the same week. Both are in good health considering they have suffered a number of strokes in recent years.

I have a friend who takes the time to regularly check on the welfare of Grant and Nancy. Their lives intertwined through tragedy.

Like the Beaumonts, Paul's life changed drastically on Australia Day in 1966. While the Beaumont parents lost their children, my friend lost his brother in a tragic water skiing accident along the Murray River.

Paul enjoys sitting and chatting with them in their separate homes. The pair may be getting on in years but both are still sharp of mind and or course alert to the regular 'chatter' from the media about the latest chapter in the search for their lost children. Paul never inquires about their painful loss but when the subject arises he listens patiently to their insights.

In late 2013, Nancy Beaumont was contacted by police concerning speculative new information about the possible burial site of her children. Authors of the book *Satin Man*, Mullins and Whiticker, caused quite a stir with their revelations regarding a possible suspect. SAPOL were about to perform an extensive dig at the 'suspects' former workplace.

The police were thoughtful and sensitive in passing on this traumatic information and were concerned about her wellbeing. Nancy later revealed, "Paul, it doesn't bother me. I can't be hurt anymore than what I have."

Sometimes Paul is asked by Mrs Beaumont to do an odd errand. A few years ago, Nancy wanted him to take a pendant into the local jewellery store to get the latch fixed. Paul could see that the pendant was old and probably not worth fixing but took it in for repair anyway.

A few weeks later, he visited Mrs Beaumont to return the repaired piece of jewellery. Her eyes lit up as the pendant had been polished and cleaned. "It's beautiful Paul; now open the latch for me."

Paul opened the heart shape pendant. Inside was a tiny and faded image of Jane, Arnna and Grant. Mrs Beaumont's moist eyes gazed at the image. Her children were with her once more. Gone but *never* forgotten.

References

Newspapers:

The Advertiser:
1947 — January 7.
1952 — September 21, 30.
1966 — January 28, 29. February 1, 3, 4, 5, 7, 10, 11, 12, 15, 16, 17, 24. March 12, 15, 17, 18. July 16. August 3, 9. September 12, 26, 27, 30. October 8, 10, 17. November 9, 10, 11, 12, 13, 15, 16, 18.
1967 — January 27. March 11, 14.
1968 — February 29.
1973 — August 27, 28, 29, 31. September 7.
1986 — March 12,13.
1988 — March 3.
1989 — February 16.
1990 — February 8, 23, 24. March 3, 17, 18. April 6, 17, May 11, 12.
1992 — May 30, June 1, 6, 23. August 6, 8. September 9. December 13.
1995 — March 28, December 16.
1996 — January 22, March 23, April 27, May 1, 5, June 24, September 9.
1997 — February 7, August 6, 7, 8.
1998 — August 19, 22, December 12.
2002 — July 23.

2005 — January 21, December 12.
2006 — October 27.
2007 — April 24, August 10, August 31, September 22.
2012 — April 17, August 14.
2013 — July 25, August 24, November 28.
2014 — September 13.
2015 — March 12, May 21, July 14.

The Argus
1925 — August 18.

The News
1953 — February 23.
1966 — January 28, 29, 31. February 2, 3, 10, 12, 17, 20, 21. March 29. April 18, 19. July 18, 20. August 1, 3, 8, 27. September 9. October 10, 12, 18, 23. November 15, 16. December 12.
1967 — March 1, 2, 10. September 5.
1968 — February 19, 20, 22, 23. March 16.

Sunday Mail
1966 — January 29. February 3, 10. September 10, 23, 30.
1967 — January 21.
1990 — March 18.
1992 — May 31.
1993 — June 17.
1998 — December 13.
2007 — April 22, 29, September 23.

Courier Mail
1985 — January 12.
1989 — February 16.

The Age
1966 — February 10.
1973 — August 27.
2007 — April 22.

Herald Sun
2006 — October 25.

Publications:

- *Inquest into the death of Joanne Ratcliffe* — 1979. S.A Coroner.
- *Crimes that shocked Australia*. Sharpe, Currawong Press, (1982).
- *Nothing But The Truth — The Life and Times of Jack 'Ace' Ayling* — Ironbark (1993).
- *Women's Weekly* — October 5, 1966.
- *The Satin Man: The Disappearance of the Beaumont Children* — Whiticker & Mullins. New Holland. (2013).
- *Journey into Darkness* — John Douglas, Mark Olshaker. Simon and Schuster. (1997).
- *The Anatomy of Motive* — Douglas, Olshaker. Scribner. (1999).
- *Mind Hunter* — Douglas, Olshaker. Scribner (1995).
- *The Sinners Club* — Tom Prior. Penguin (1993).
- *The Forgotten Crime — The Adelaide Oval Abductions* — Michael Madigan — New Holland Publishing (unpublished).
- *Searching for the Beaumont Children: Australia's Most Famous Unsolved Mystery*. Alan Whiticker, (2006). John Wiley & Sons Australia.
- *Young Blood: the Story of the Family Murders*. Robert (Bob) O'Brien. (2002). Harper Collins.
- *Deadline*. Alan Dower. (1979) Hutchinson.

Index

A

Adelaide Oval 133, 139, 140, 142, 143, 144, 146, 151, 158, 159, 161, 164, 174, 176, 194, 197, 199, 200, 215, 217, 218, 219, 241, 247, 250
Adelaide's Today Tonight 211, 214
Anderson, Ken 71, 72, 107, 194
Anzac Day 19
Archer, Graham 4, 214, 250
Ayling, Jack 62, 63, 64, 74, 247

B

Babes in the Ditch Murder 70
Ballis, Douglas 76, 77
Barnes, Alan 165, 173, 175, 250
Barossa Valley 81
Bay Sheffield 224
Beaumont children 3, 16, 17, 21, 22, 23, 24, 26, 31, 39, 47, 48, 50, 51, 53, 60, 61, 72, 74, 99, 108, 121, 125, 126, 130, 188, 230, 236, 244

Beaumont, Max 66
Bignell, Leon 178, 179, 250
Blackwell, Barry 88, 89, 91, 237, 250
Blight, Detective 36, 43, 49, 50, 104, 105, 121, 213
Boundary Road 56
Bradley, Stephen Leslie 54, 55
Bray, Des (Det. Superintendent) 212, 240, 250
Bridgart, Leigh Anthony 200, 250
Brighton Road 24, 56, 94, 112
Broadway, The 110
Brook, Simon 205, 206
Brown, Arthur 198
Burns, Gary (Police Commissioner) 240

C

Castalloy 211, 212, 213, 250
Church, Frank 188
Citizens Action Committee 98, 99
City Meat Company 21
Clements, Peggy 167, 168, 250

Colley Reserve 26
Collins, Ruth 222, 247, 250
Coober Pedy 204
Coulthart, Ross 196
Coward, Mike 105
Crameri, Tony. (Major Crime Superintendent) 193
Crease, Janet 189
Crease, Kevin 41, 189
Creswell Stand 136, 137, 143, 145
Croiset, Gerald 84, 85, 86, 87, 88, 90, 91, 92, 93, 94, 95, 96, 97, 98, 99, 158, 159, 160, 187
Croiset, Gerard Jnr 158
Crypt (Minda Home) 87
Czarnecki, Peter von 44

D

Dandenong Letters 118, 119, 120, 121, 122, 123, 124, 125, 178, 181, 182, 251
Davie, Gordon 202, 203, 204, 251
Devon cargo ship 129
Diagonal Road 24, 25, 34, 112, 230
Dickson, Paul (Ass. Commissioner) 213
DNA 155, 185, 187
Doherty, John 147, 148, 251
Douglas, John 192, 226, 247
Dower, Alan 118, 247, 251
Duncan, Dr. George 156, 157, 251
Dunn, Raymond Lawrence 67
Dunstan, Donald (SA Premier) 156, 251
Dykshoorn, Marinus 100

E

Easom, Doug 107
Ellis, Nancy 21, 22, 23, 32
Engelhardt, Laura 231
Exclusive Brethren 73

F

Family Murders 175
FBI 191, 192, 225, 226, 227, 251
Fort Largs Police Academy 40
Francis, Brian 107

G

Glenelg Beach 16, 23, 25, 26, 31, 70, 140, 220, 238
Glenelg Police Station 26, 32, 37, 41, 45, 49, 234, 251
Glenside Hospital 106
Gollan, Detective 69
Gordon, Greg and Christine 146
Gordon, Kirste 134, 164, 173, 174, 193, 197, 199, 215, 237
Gordon, Ray 64
Gregory, Daphne 55
Grose, Ron 73, 74
Grosser, Erwin Erhardt 66, 67

H

Hallett Cove 68
Harding Street 16, 27, 34, 51, 71, 230
Harrison, Ted 53
Hart, Stanley 217, 218, 219, 251
Hattam, Mary Olive 238, 239, 251
Hayes, Bill 212
Hendrickson, Dr 88, 91
Hill, Laurel 166, 167

Index

Hills, Ben 18, 78, 100, 151, 152, 251
Hoax calls 66, 75, 152, 182
Holdfast Bay Sailing Club 35
Holland, Det. Inspector 75
Holt, Harold (Prime Minister) 127
Huckel, Mrs Ruth 134, 139, 141, 142, 251
Huckel, Rita 134
Hunt, Nigel 193, 194, 214
Hutchins, Greg 216
Hutchins, Greg (Det. Inspector) 216, 251

J

James, Jimmy 79
James, Roger 156
Jetty Road 26, 34, 69, 92

K

Kaniva 73, 75
Kelly, Ray 54, 55, 56, 57, 58, 232
Kelvin, Richard 165, 176, 191
Kilmartin, Anthony & Robert 134, 135, 136, 137, 144, 251
Kipling, Trevor (Detective) 194, 195, 251
Kirk, Stacey Lee 239
Kroeger, John 118, 119, 251

L

Langley, Mark 165, 173, 175, 251
Lanning, Ken 226, 227, 228, 251
Laurie, Sue 197
Leane, Deputy Commissioner 94
Lehmann, Det. Col 141, 143, 144, 148, 155, 251
Lenton, Superintendent Noel 46, 55, 58, 121, 146
Linge, Kenneth 196
Little Women 31
Littley, Bryan 215, 217, 218, 219, 220, 222, 252
Loof, Karel 85

M

MacKay, Susan & Judith 198
Marino 81
Marshall, Mark 216, 217
Mathieson, Alec 152, 252
Matters, Moss 50, 213, 234
McCall, John Louis (Det. Sgt.) 154
McGeorge, Dr George 61, 62
McIntyre, Maxwell 220, 221, 222, 252
McKinna, Police Commissioner 121
McPherson, Lenny 55
Miller, James 164, 165
Minda Home 86
Moodoo, Daniel 79
Morros, Raymond 183, 252
Moseley Square 26, 31, 32
Moseley Street, 34, 104, 112
Mr B 173, 174, 176, 177, 191, 193, 252
Mr X 219, 220, 221, 252
Mud Islands 128
Mueller, Helmut 81, 82
Muir, Neil 165, 252
Mullighan Inquiry 215
Mullighan, Ted 215, 218, 237, 252
Mullins, Stuart 208, 209, 210, 211, 212, 244, 247, 252
Munro, I 34
Murdoch, Rupert 239
Myponga 173, 176, 177, 252

N

Nikola, Det. Sgt. 171
Nuriootpa 67

O

O'Brien, Robert (Detective) 194
Occam's Razor 230
O'Neill, James 200, 201, 202, 203,
One pound note 104, 105, 209, 213, 232

P

Palmer, Det. A. 39, 68, 69
Paringa Park Primary School 53, 58
Paringa warehouse 99
Parker, Alice 122, 123
Patawalonga Boat Haven 40
Patterson, Tom 34, 37, 56, 231, 232
Percy, Derek 197, 204, 205, 206, 207
Pfeiffer, Wendy 78, 80
Phipps, Harry 211, 212, 213, 252
Pier Hotel 42, 92
Plymouth Brethren 103
Polites, Con 90, 91, 92, 93, 94, 95, 187, 188, 189, 252
Port Pirie 90
Port Road,Thebarton 145
Port Wakefield 158
Prior, Tom 48, 101, 149, 150, 247

R

Ratcliffe, Joanne 133, 134, 135, 136, 138, 139, 140, 141, 143, 147, 148, 149, 150, 155, 158, 160, 161, 162, 164, 173, 174, 176, 193, 195, 197, 199, 200, 215, 216, 217, 218, 237, 247, 252
Redston, Alan 205, 252
Reynolds, Margaret 70
River Murray Caledonian Society. 142
Ryan, Ronald 55

S

Sacred Heart College 84
Salter, Dr 69
Satin Man, The 211
Schmidt, Marianne 35, 205
Schouten, John 187
Schramm, Paul (Superintendent) 200, 252
Scotland Yard 70, 130, 155, 156, 184
Sea Rescue Squadron 29
Semler, Dean 41
Sharrock, Christine 35, 205
Silvester, John 204, 253
Sir Edwin Smith Stand 143, 158
Slee, Max 40
Smith, Ricky John 201
Smithson, Mike 190, 191, 253
Snowtown, 18
Somerton Park 16, 25, 37, 55, 56, 83, 96, 100, 104, 109, 149, 230
Somerton Park Brownies 83
Stansbury, Bert 118, 253

Steele, Douglas 118, 123, 253
Stillwell, Linda 129, 253
Stogneff, Peter 165, 253
Stokes, Doris 160, 161, 162, 253
Stuart, Kenneth Charles 168
Stuart, Rupert Maxwell 238
Suburban Taxis 19, 33
'Sunday Night' Seven Network 196
Super Sleuth 154, 155, 253
Swaine, Det. Stan 74, 79, 105, 119, 120, 121, 122, 123, 124, 182, 183, 184, 185, 186, 187, 253
Swan, Brian (Sergeant) 207

T

Taylor, Brian 73
The Truth 62
Thorne, Graeme 54, 55, 61
Torrens Parade Ground 11, 18
Torrens River 133, 161
Trevelion, Doug 87, 253
Truro Murders 165, 253
Tuohy, Yvonne Elizabeth 204
Turner, James 183, 184, 253

V

Veale Gardens 90, 237, 253
Von , Bevan Spencer 157, 166, 173, 174, 176, 177, 180, 190, 191, 192, 193, 194, 195, 196, 197
Von Czarnecki, Peter 44

W

Walker, Peter John 55
Wallach, Susan 78
Walsh, Frank (SA Premier) 97
Wanda Murders 35, 205
Washington AG 229
Watsonia 18
Weimaraner dogs 189
Wenzel's 104, 209, 231, 253
Whiticker, Alan 208, 209, 211, 212, 244, 247, 253
Widgery, Janine 202, 253
Wilson, Bruce 201
Wilton Avenue 94, 96, 188
Wohling, Mr Ken 136, 144, 253
Woodside Army Barracks 18
Woolcocks Discount House 98
Wordley, Dick 118, 158, 253
Worrell, Christopher 164, 165, 253

Y

Yatina 215, 216, 217, 219, 253

Z

Zeunert, Detective 95

www.ingramcontent.com/pod-product-compliance
Lightning Source LLC
Chambersburg PA
CBHW032038150426
43194CB00006B/335